Bradford Libraries

C C L

B18

CW0764451

City of Bradford Metropolitan District Council

www.bradford.gov.uk

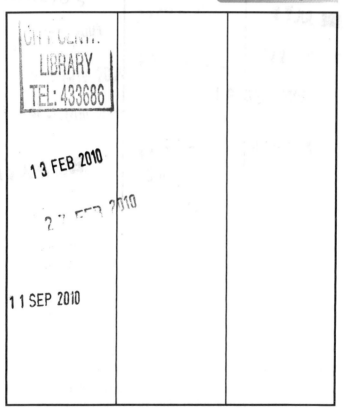

CITY CENTR.
LIBRARY
TEL: 433686

1 3 FEB 2010

2 .. FEB 2010

1 1 SEP 2010

CEN
BOO

Please return/renew this item by the last date shown. Items not required by other customers may be renewed by phone and over the internet.

First published in 2003

Copyright © Abdullah Saeed 2003

Abdullah Saeed is Associate Professor and Head of the Arabic and Islamic Studies Program at the Melbourne Institute of Asian Languages and Societies, University of Melbourne. Among his recent publications are *Islamic Banking and Interest* (1999), *Muslim Communities in Australia* (co-edited, 2001) and *Freedom of Religion, Apostasy and Islam* (co-authored, 2003).

All rights reserved. No part of this book may be reproduced or transmitted in any form or by any means, electronic or mechanical, including photocopying, recording or by any information storage and retrieval system, without prior permission in writing from the publisher. The *Australian Copyright Act 1968* (the Act) allows a maximum of one chapter or 10 per cent of this book, whichever is the greater, to be photocopied by any educational institution for its educational purposes provided that the educational institution (or body that administers it) has given a remuneration notice to Copyright Agency Limited (CAL) under the Act.

Allen & Unwin
83 Alexander Street
Crows Nest NSW 2065
Australia
Phone: (61 2) 8425 0100
Fax: (61 2) 9906 2218
Email: info@allenandunwin.com
Web: www.allenandunwin.com

National Library of Australia
Cataloguing-in-Publication entry:

Saeed, Abdullah.
  Islam in Australia.

  ISBN 1 86508 864 1 (pbk).

  1. Islam - Australia. I. Title.

297.0994

BRADFORD METROPOLITAN DISTRICT LIBRARIES		
Askews	13-Nov-2003	
297.0994	£7.99	
LEN		

Text design by Alex Nahlous and Simon Paterson
Indexer: Russell Brooks
Set in 11/15 pt Centaur MT by Bookhouse, Sydney
Printed by Griffin Press, South Australia

10 9 8 7 6 5 4 3 2 1

CONTENTS

INTRODUCTION

In the aftermath of September 11, 2001 and in light of the increasing number of asylum seekers landing on our shores during the past few years, a heated debate began in Australia—in newspapers, over talkback radio and even on television—about the presence of Islam and Muslims in Australia. Some argued that it is time for us to take a hard look at Islam and the potential threat it poses to Australia, its society and values. Others argued that such a generalisation is untenable given the enormous diversity of Muslim people and Islamic practice—one cannot put all 1200 million Muslims of the world in one basket and label them all as terrorists. In this debate, Muslims were often put on the defensive. Their basic beliefs, values and norms and religious institutions suddenly became the focus of the media and even Australian security services. 'Islam' and 'Muslim' became problematic labels. Islamic symbols became the target of much hatred, which was often directed at Muslims, by a small but vocal segment of Australian society. There were also a number of documented cases of violence against Muslims in the community.

As the scale of events in New York and Washington unfolded and the Muslim involvement in the attacks became increasingly clear, many Australians, particularly those who had not previously been in contact with Muslim communities here or abroad, naturally became suspicious of both Islam and Muslims. Muslims had to explain what Islam meant to them, and particularly in the context of Australian life. They had to demystify concepts like *jihad* and *hijab* and to convince an increasingly sceptical audience that Islam itself is not to blame for the atrocities committed by extremists and radicals among them. It was in this context that I was asked by the late John Iremonger of Allen & Unwin to write a short and accessible book on Islam with a high degree of emphasis on Islam as lived in Australia, a book that would explain the basic beliefs, values and institutions of Islam while highlighting the experience of Muslims in Australia.

While it is relatively easy to write an introduction to Islam, it is extremely difficult to contextualise Islam within Australia. Part of the problem is this: Islam is not one thing, as is commonly thought. Islam is perceived and lived in many different ways by Muslims around the world. It is true that there are certain fundamental ideas, beliefs, practices and values which are common to all Muslims, but as in most religions that are practised in many different countries, they are relatively few. Muslims frequently disagree on interpretation and detail. They have, like any other religious tradition, many theological orientations, legal schools and religio-political divisions. They have their fair share of conservatives, liberals, traditionalists, modernists and post-modernists.

Muslims are one of the most ethnically diverse religious groups in Australia. Australian Muslims come from almost all corners of the world, bringing with them from their home countries linguistic and cultural differences as well as their various interpretations of Islam. Complicating this further is the fact that more than 36 per cent of Australian Muslims are born and bred in this country and that their experience of Islam is within the Australian context—many are converts to Islam from European and other backgrounds, while others are second, third and even fourth generation Muslim Australians for whom there is no other 'home'. Dealing with this cultural, linguistic and religious diversity is one of the most challenging tasks for anyone interested in writing an introductory on a topic like 'Islam in Australia'. Certainly, such an introduction cannot avoid some of the generalisations and overly simplistic statements which may or may not apply to all Australian Muslims and the writer will have to commit a few such academic sins in the interest of keeping the material simple and accessible.

Much of what has been written on Islam in Australia focuses on certain ethnicities, like the Lebanese community or the Turkish community, often from a sociological perspective. Very few texts deal directly with understanding 'Islam' in Australia and at an accessible level. The need for such a general text is acute.

This book is intended for a general readership and attempts to give the reader a general understanding of Islam and the Muslim community life in Australia. It also highlights some of the institutional developments in the Muslim communities in Australia, as well as some of the concerns and challenges Australian Muslims face, without going into in-depth analysis of any particular aspect. Such treatment can be found in a number of scholarly texts on various aspects of life in Australia, such as the reference work *The Australian People*.

The book attempts to avoid jargon, footnotes and references to specific people or organisations as much as possible. Often it refers to trends such as Traditionalists, neo-Modernists, neo-Revivalists and Liberals within Islam without giving any specific names among Australian Muslims who may or may not belong to these trends. Its interest is in providing an overview, a general understanding of the issues, and in highlighting some of the complexities associated with specific issues.

I have benefited enormously from the works written on the topic. In particular, I have used extensively *The Australian People* (edited by James Jupp), particularly for Chapter I. Much of the information in that chapter comes from this source. Although it is difficult to list here all sources I have used and benefited from, many are listed in the Bibliography in this book.

I have attempted to show the pragmatism of Australian Muslims, their efforts to be part of the Australian society, and their attempts to negotiate some of the challenges they face as Muslims. Throughout the book I emphasise the diversity that exists among Muslims, not the unity which some Muslims tend to focus on.

I hope that this book will contribute to our understanding of one of the most misunderstood religions in the world and the complexities associated with the Muslim community, its diversity and unity, its struggle to remain an element of the Australian fabric of society.

I would like to thank a number of colleagues, friends and others for contributing significantly to the development of this book. In particular I would like to thank Rachel Woodlock, who read and polished the draft manuscript quite thoroughly and helped me include some of the specific information I needed about the Muslim communities. Her contributions enriched the book in many ways. She also helped me obtain several people's personal stories which are included here. I also thank the late John Iremonger of Allen & Unwin for his critical reading of the early draft of the book and his penetrating comments and suggestions for revising the manuscript in order to 'Australianise' the text, which certainly helped transform the original manuscript in a significant way. We are deeply saddened by the untimely death of John who would have liked to see this project completed. I thank Alexandra Nahlous of Allen & Unwin for her very helpful comments and suggestions as well as the editorial support she kindly gave me; Robyn Flemming for copyediting the text; Bilal Cleland, who himself recently published a book on the history of Muslims in Australia; Shahram Akbarzadeh, with whom I edited *Muslim Communities in Australia* (UNSW Press, 2001); Yusuf Eades, Erin Dolan and Abdul Ghafoor Abdul Raheem for their comments and suggestions; and all those whose 'personal stories' are included in this book. Finally, I thank my wife and my son for their patience and support throughout the project.

Chapter 1

WHO ARE AUSTRALIA'S MUSLIMS?

Australia's Muslims are a diverse group of people, coming from more than 70 different countries. They come from practically every corner of the world: from the Middle East, Russia, Europe, the Indian subcontinent, Africa, Southeast Asia and even China. They speak languages ranging from English, Arabic, Turkish, Persian and Bosnian to Chinese, Tamil, Italian, German, French, Greek, Croatian, Thai, Vietnamese, Serbian, Spanish, Russian, Maltese and Hungarian. While the vast majority of Muslims speak English, the largest non-English language spoken by Muslims is Arabic, followed by Turkish.

The number of Australian Muslims recorded in the 2001 Census was 281 572 (approximately 1.5 per cent of the total population), of whom approximately 53 per cent were male and

47 per cent were female. While the majority were born overseas, mainly in countries like Lebanon, Turkey, Afghanistan, Bosnia, Pakistan, Indonesia, Iraq, Bangladesh and Iran, the single largest bloc of Australian Muslims are Australian-born, representing 36.5 per cent of the Muslim population. It is a relatively young population: 50 per cent are under the age of 24.

The vast majority of Muslims live in Sydney and Melbourne. In Sydney the most popular suburbs are Auburn, Greenacre, Bankstown, Lakemba and Punchbowl. In Melbourne, Muslims tend to live in Meadow Heights, Reservoir, Dallas, Noble Park and Coburg. Relatively small numbers live in the other state and territory capitals, as well as outside the capital cities, for example in Shepparton in northern Victoria.

The majority of the Muslim population is working class. Only 27 per cent are in the categories of professionals, managers and administrators and technicians. The rest (73 per cent) are employed as clerical, service and transport workers, tradespersons and labourers. In each of these two broad categories, women represent approximately one-third of workers, which is in line with the general Australian population. Unemployment among certain ethnic groups, in particular those who are unskilled and without English language skills, is high. Muslims from some ethnic groups, such as those from India, Pakistan, Bangladesh and Egypt, do better in terms of occupation and weekly income, as most are skilled migrants and relatively recent arrivals.

Most Muslims in Australia are Sunni but there is a significant minority of Shi'a as well. Several sects (some of which are not considered Muslim by the mainstream Muslim community) are also represented, for example Bektashis, Ahmadis, Alawis and

Druse. Since the Census does not make distinctions between these groups, it is difficult to estimate their numbers.

MUSLIM MIGRANTS TO AUSTRALIA

A number of Australia's northern neighbours are Muslim. Islam arrived into Southeast Asia as early as the beginning of the eighth century CE.[1] From then on, its growth and spread continued. By the twelfth century, Islam was an important religion in parts of what we call today Malaysia and Indonesia. Today, Australia's closest neighbour, Indonesia, is the world's largest Muslim-majority country. Other Muslim-majority countries in the region are Malaysia and Brunei. Significant Muslim minorities exist in the Philippines, Thailand and China.

MACASSANS

The first Muslims to come into contact with Australia predate European settlement, with visits from Macassan fishermen from around the 1750s onwards. From Macassar in southern Sulawesi, part of today's Indonesia, fishermen would visit the coast of northern Australia annually in order to catch a particular type of sea slug called the trepang. Bilal Cleland writes:

Each year in December, as the low pressure cell moved over Australia and the winds blew towards the south, the prahus [boats] left Macassar for camps along the shores of Marege. Then four months later, as the sun moved over the northern hemisphere and the winds blew from the continent towards the northern equatorial zone, they sailed back. By May they had all gone. While they were here they caught, cooked and dried the sea slug or trepang in beach camps.[2]

On their travels, these Macassan fishermen met Aboriginal people from the north of Australia, even influencing the local languages. (Macassan loan words include *balanda*: white man, and *rupiah*: money.)

Unlike European contact, the encounters between the Macassans and the Aboriginal people were generally peaceful and friendly. For over 150 years, these Muslims visited Australia, but with European control of the island continent came restrictions on Macassans entering Australian territorial waters. Imposition of heavy customs duties, the introduction of the *Immigration Restriction Act 1901* and restriction of access for Macassans to some ports in the north led to the cessation of their annual visits by 1907.

Below is an overview of six Muslim communities in Australia. These communities were chosen because, according to the 2001 Census, by place of birth they are the largest in number (with the exception of those born in Australia): Lebanese, Turks, Afghans, Bosnians, Pakistanis and Indonesians. Given that the Afghans were the first Muslim migrants, they will be dealt with first and in some detail. Others will be dealt with briefly.

AFGHANS[3]

A few Muslims came to Australia as part of European settlement, arriving as sailors on British ships, who were subsequently stranded, or as convicts during the period of penal settlement. However, it was the adoption of camel transport that saw

Muslims arrive in somewhat greater numbers. The new settlers in Australia needed a method of travelling the vast deserts of the interior. Horses and bullocks, which were used in the past for such tasks, were not suited to the harsh outback conditions where water was scarce and temperatures extremely high. Camels were suggested as a way of conducting expeditions and moving goods from one part of the country to another. For this purpose, Governor Gawler of South Australia requested the purchase of six camels; however, only one actually survived the sea journey, arriving in Adelaide in 1840 from the Indian subcontinent. In 1860, the Victorian government imported 24 camels from India. Along with them came three Afghans as camel drivers. These Afghans and the camels became part of the Burke and Wills expedition team. In 1865, Thomas Elder from South Australia imported 124 camels with 31 Afghan camel drivers. From then on, more camels began to be imported. Most of the Afghans who came to Australia as camel drivers were from the Pashtun tribes of today's Pakistan and Afghanistan, and were generally referred to as 'Afghans'.

By the 1880s and 1890s, Afghans more or less controlled the camel transport business in New South Wales, Queensland, South Australia, Western Australia and Central Australia. Many lived in small towns called Ghan towns. By 1901, there were 600 camel drivers, just under half of whom were born in Afghanistan; the remainder were from areas of modern Pakistan.

Afghans played a largely unrecognised part in the major explorations and expeditions of the day. In 1896, two Afghans, Bejah Dervish and Said Ameer, accompanied the Albert Calvert Expedition. When two of the European explorers went missing, the Afghans searched for them for days in terrible conditions and eventually died of starvation. Bejah Dervish's son, Abdul 'Jack' Dervish, was part of the last major exploration of the interior: the 1939 Madigan Expedition across the Simpson Desert. Today there still exist a few places named after the Afghan pioneers, such as Bejah Hill and Saleh's Fish Pond.

At its peak, approximately 3000 Afghans were working as camel drivers across Australia. These early Muslim settlers were mostly men who travelled to Australia without their families, hoping one day to return to their homelands. Some returned to what are today Pakistan and Afghanistan. Others who found it difficult to return stayed permanently in Australia. As was the case for all non-whites at the time, life was not easy for these men. They were often marginalised and considered inferior to the dominant Christian white Europeans. Nevertheless, some appear to have done well despite the prejudice, even becoming relatively wealthy and influential. But such individuals were few and far between. Issues of race, religion and economic handicap maintained the marginalisation, and those who decided to stay in Australia could usually find wives only among the disadvantaged women of the community: either detribalised Aboriginal women or deserted wives of others.

When Australia was federated in 1901, legislation was introduced to restrict non-white immigration and citizenship. The 1920s then saw the end of the camel transport industry with the arrival of new modes of mechanised transport such as the automobile. The combined effect of the White Australia Policy, racism and loss of employment opportunities as a result of the decimation of the camel transport industry meant that many

Afghans had to leave Australia. Those who fought to stay battled administrative red tape with little success, as the discriminatory White Australia Policy remained in place until its formal abolition by the Whitlam government in 1972.

Afghans began to migrate to Australia again from the late 1970s onwards. Since 1980, the number of Afghan refugees arriving in Australia increased to an average of 500 every year, reaching almost 1000 in 1991–92. In 2001, there were 9923 Australians born in Afghanistan. Many in this wave of Afghan migrants are from middle-class backgrounds in Afghanistan. Most live in Sydney and Melbourne and they have established a number of socieities and mosques.

LEBANESE[4]

Lebanese migration to Australia began in the late nineteenth century and continued throughout the twentieth century. Most early Lebanese migrants were Christian. Lebanese Muslim migration in large numbers began relatively late, particularly in the post-1975 period. By 2001, there were 29 321 Lebanese-born Muslims in Australia. Of these, two-thirds lived in Sydney; most of the remaining third lived in Melbourne. The majority of Lebanese Muslims are Sunni; a third are Shi'a and there are relatively small numbers of Druse and Alawis.

In Australia, the Lebanese Muslim sects not only observe their own religious practices and beliefs but also maintain separate institutions and exist as distinct sectarian communities in major cities. These sectarian tendencies, which were inherited from the sectarian history of Lebanon in the twentieth century and the conflicts there in the 1970s, have become less vigorous as the Lebanese Muslim communities have become established, and as a result of their interaction with other Australian Muslims. This is also facilitated by the ongoing experience of discrimination against other Muslims in fighting racism and prejudice, and for their religious and cultural rights, such as establishing mosques.

Lebanese Muslims of Sunni background established the Lebanese Muslim Association in Sydney in 1956. They also built the Imam Ali mosque in Lakemba (known today as the Lakemba mosque), which was completed in 1976 and to this day, remains associated with the Lebanese Sunni Muslim community. Many Lebanese Muslims of Shi'a background also settled in Sydney, around the area of Arncliffe. The al-Zahra mosque was built in Arncliffe in 1983 for this community. In Melbourne, many Lebanese Muslims live in the suburbs of Moreland, Preston and Brunswick. Although Muslims may attend any mosque, some mosques in Melbourne—such as those at Preston, Newport, Fawkner and Maidstone—are attended by a large number of Lebanese.

TURKS[5]

The existence of Turkish-born people in Australia dates back to the early nineteenth century. By 1911, they numbered around 300, but following the First World War, in which Australians and Turks (Ottomans) fought each other, the number of Turkish-born people in Australia declined. In 1967, the Australian government negotiated an agreement with Turkey under which Australia was to receive Turkish migrants at a time when European migration to Australia was declining. Since the government was interested in migrants who would settle in Australia permanently, it gave preference to married couples and family units that included young children. By 2001, the number of Turkish-born Muslims in Australia numbered 23 479.

The migrants from Turkey in the 1960s came largely from rural backgrounds, but many worked in factories upon their arrival. At the time, approximately 30 per cent were rated as skilled and 70 per cent unskilled. This changed in the 1980s when skilled Turks began to apply to enter Australia as independent migrants. They spoke English and had professional qualifications. By the turn of the century, immigration from Turkey had almost ceased.

The vast majoritiy of Turkish Muslims are Sunni. More than 90 per cent of Turkish-born people live in Victoria and New South Wales, mainly in Melbourne and Sydney. In Melbourne, they reside largely in suburbs such as Broadmeadows, Collingwood, Brunswick, Coburg, Fitzroy, Richmond, Springvale and Dandenong. In Sydney, they are concentrated in Auburn, Botany, Fairfield, Marrickville, Blacktown and Ashfield.

BOSNIANS[6]

In the wake of the civil war in the former Yugoslavia in the 1990s, more than 1 million Bosnians were displaced. Of those, Australia accepted several thousand. In 2001, the Bosnian-born Muslim population of Australia was 9892. They live mainly in suburbs close to industrial/working-class areas such as Dandenong, Broadmeadows, Preston and Brunswick in Melbourne, and

Auburn in Sydney. When they arrived in Australia, many Bosnians spoke little English and therefore had difficulty finding employment. Relatively few worked in middle-class occupations. Of those who did find work, most were employed as factory workers.

PAKISTANIS[7]

Pakistani migration to Australia (if we exclude the Afghans who came earlier from parts of what is now modern Pakistan) began in the 1960s after the easing of restrictions on Asian migration. Pakistani migrants were mostly highly educated and came from middle- or upper-middle-class families. By 2001, there were 9238 Pakistani-born Australian Muslims.

Pakistanis live mostly in Sydney and Melbourne. The cultural, linguistic, ethnic and religious diversity in modern Pakistan is reflected in the Australian Pakistani community. Pakistani Muslims, though representing only 3 per cent of Australian Muslims, play a significant and sometimes dominant role in Australian Muslim organisations such as Islamic councils. This role can be attributed to their educational, economic and occupational status. Pakistanis find it relatively easy to integrate into the mainstream Australian community, mainly because of their economic, social and educational background, and also because of their love of sport such as cricket, hockey and squash, which they share with Anglo-Australians. However, Pakistanis are keen to maintain their ethnic and national identities through Urdu language maintenance, religious education and food, as well as through arranged marriages.

INDONESIANS[8]

Apart from the Macassar fishermen who came to Australia on a temporary basis until the early twentieth century, 'Indonesians' (from Kupang and Java) were brought to work in the pearling industry and sugar plantations in the late nineteenth century. With the immigration restrictions of 1901, most returned to their homeland and only a small number remained in Australia. It was only in the 1950s and 1960s that Indonesian students were brought to Australia as part of the Australian government's scholarship program to train them in Australian universities. During this period, some Indonesians came to Australia to teach the Indonesian language. Those who chose to settle in Australia during this period formed the nucleus of the Indonesian Muslim community. With the easing of restrictions on non-white migration in 1966, Indonesian migration to Australia increased. In addition to those who migrated permanently to Australia during the 1980s and 1990s, a large number of wealthy Indonesians sent their children to study in Australia.

Today, most Indonesians live in Sydney, followed by Melbourne, Perth and Brisbane. Although Indonesia is the world's largest Muslim majority country, only 17 per cent of Indonesian Australians consider themselves to be Muslim. Generally speaking, Indonesians have found it relatively easy to integrate into Australian society. They tend to attend mosques established by other ethnic groups.

The table on page 12 shows the 25 most important birthplaces for Australian Muslims and the percentage of Muslims from that birthplace.

Rank	Country	Total Muslims	Total Australians	% of Muslims to Total Australians
1	Australia	102 566	13 629 700	0.75
2	Lebanon	29 321	71 349	41.10
3	Turkey	23 479	29 821	78.73
4	Afghanistan	9 923	11 296	87.85
5	Bosnia and Herzegovina	9 892	23 848	41.48
6	Pakistan	9 238	11 917	77.52
7	Indonesia	8 087	47 158	17.15
8	Iraq	7 749	24 832	31.21
9	Bangladesh	7 596	9 078	83.67
10	Iran	6 353	18 789	33.81
11	Fiji	5 772	44 261	13.04
12	Cyprus	3 708	19 482	19.03
13	Somalia	3 585	3 713	96.55
14	Egypt	3 061	33 432	9.16
15	Malaysia	2 975	78 858	3.77
16	India	2 819	95 452	2.95
17	Former Yugoslav Republic of Macedonia	2 601	43 527	5.98
18	Syria	2 261	6 710	33.70
19	Yugoslavia, Federal Republic of	2 152	55 365	3.89
20	Singapore	2 091	33 485	6.24
21	South Africa	2 060	79 425	2.59
22	Kuwait	1 610	2 436	66.09
23	United Kingdom	1 410	1 036 245	0.14
24	Jordan	1 348	3 332	40.46
25	Sri Lanka	1 173	53 461	2.19
	All Other	28 742	3 505 375	0.82
	Total	281 572	1.9E+07	1.48

Source: ABS 2001 Census of Population and Housing: Muslim Community Profile: Birthplace of individual: Top 25 (based on total Muslim population).
© Commonwealth of Australia 2002

Chapter 2

THE STORY OF ISLAM AND ISLAMIC CIVILISATION

Islam—like Christianity, Judaism, Buddhism and Hinduism— is one of the major world religions today. It is followed by approximately 1200 million people in the Middle East, Asia, Africa, Europe, the Americas and Australasia. Muslims come from almost every conceivable ethnicity and culture. In fact, Muslims live in almost all countries of the world, including more than 56 states where they make up the majority of the population—that is, approximately one-quarter of all the countries in the world.

But what is the story of Islam? How did it begin, and how did it develop into the major world religion that it is today? To answer these questions we need to go back in time to the late sixth century CE. The birthplace of Islam was the Arabian Peninsula, located in West Asia, close to Africa and Europe.

In particular, Islam began in the town of Mecca, which is in present-day Saudi Arabia.

Wherever Muslims live, this story of Islam is important for them. The story is told and retold to Muslim children remarkably consistently throughout the world. Beliefs associated with the story are held by Muslims everywhere, including Australian Muslims.

THE ORIGINS OF MECCA, ACCORDING TO MUSLIM BELIEF

In the early sixth century CE, Mecca was already an ancient town whose inhabitants' main form of business was the caravan trade. Muslims believe that Mecca originated centuries earlier with the Prophet Abraham and his son Ishmael. Abraham's wife Hagar, had given birth to Ishmael and later, after Abraham's first wife Sarah bore him Isaac, there were difficulties between the two women. Eventually, Abraham had to take Hagar and Ishmael away from their home town, leaving them in what became known as Mecca—a barren place with no water, trees or settlements. In this harsh environment, Hagar and Ishmael were struggling to find food and water when, according to Muslim belief, miraculously water began to gush forth from a place later called Zamzam which still provides water today. Because of the water, people came from other parts of Arabia and settled, leading to the establishment of Mecca. Ishmael is believed to have grown up in Mecca and married a woman who had settled there; thus, he is considered the ancestor of the North Arabian tribes.

The connection between Abraham and Muhammad, the Prophet of Islam, is rooted in the latter's descent through

Abraham's son, Ishmael. Furthermore, the sanctuary of the Ka'ba (a cube-shaped building now located within the Grand Mosque in Mecca) which Muslims revere and turn towards at least five times a day in their prayers, is believed to have been originally built by Abraham and Ishmael. Therefore, the heartland of Islam is not only connected to Muhammad, but also to Abraham and his family through Ishmael.

For Muslims, Islam is closely connected to the prophets whose stories appear in the Hebrew scriptures and Christianity's Old Testament. Stories of biblical figures such as Noah, Abraham, Isaac, Ishmael, Jacob, Joseph, Lot, Moses, Aaron, Ezekiel, Elias, Jonah, Zechariah, David and Solomon have been told and retold in Muslim communities around the world since Islam emerged in the early seventh century. For a Muslim, there is a close relationship between Islam and the biblical prophets: they taught essentially the same message which Muhammad taught to his people—that is, the belief in one God. From a Muslim perspective, Judaism, Christianity and Islam all share many more common ideas, beliefs, values and institutions than is generally understood.

Mecca and the caravan trade

The scarcity of arable land meant that Mecca did not have any agriculture of note. Meccans, therefore, had to rely on other forms of livelihood. In the sixth century, they appear to have been engaged in buying, selling and transporting goods between southern and northern Arabia using camels as a means of transport. Through this trade activity, many Meccans became relatively rich. Mecca was also home to the religious sanctuary, Ka'ba, which many Arabs visited. Muslims believe that this pilgrimage of pre-Islamic Arabs was a modified version of Abraham and Ishmael's pilgrimage. The pilgrimage of pre-Islamic Arabs also meant, for Meccans, opportunities for trade. Mecca thus became an important commercial town in the western part of Arabia even before the emergence of Islam.

Compared to the nomadic tribes of the region, the more settled Mecca, with its caravan trade, was relatively well off. Its society, like the rest of Arabia, was composed of clans and tribes, with one in particular dominating Mecca—the Quraysh—with its several clans made up of various families, some of whom were prominent in trade, or in political or religious affairs.

Religious and cultural life

Mecca's religious life appears to have been richly composed of a number of diverse belief systems. In Mecca itself, locals believed in a variety of deities. Some believed in one god without subscribing to any particular religious affiliation. There is evidence to suggest that some other Meccans were Christian and, possibly, Jewish. There were significant numbers of Christians and Jews in Arabia, and often they would travel on business to Mecca where they would meet and mix with the local population.

In Mecca, religious concepts and ideas such as 'God', 'Creator', 'Prophet', 'Scripture' and 'Angel' were reasonably well known. Muslim tradition holds that knowledge of these ideas goes back to the teachings of Abraham and, in particular, of

Ishmael, who is believed to have lived and taught about these matters in Mecca. However, after Ishmael's death, much of his teachings were distorted, and instead of the monotheism (belief in the existence of one God) that he taught, polytheism (belief in the existence of more than one God) spread. By the time Islam emerged, there remained very few traces of the religion of Abraham and Ishmael in Mecca.

Another aspect of Meccan life was the importance given to their Arabic tongue, particularly the art of poetry. Possessing an oral culture, the Meccans appreciated the power of language. The poet of a clan became its spokesperson, whose poetry would be memorised and passed on to others. During important trading and religious occasions, festivals were held in and around Mecca in which poetry recitations and competitions were held.

By the early seventh century, the Arabic language as we know it today was widely used in Mecca, Medina and much of northern Arabia. (Southern Arabia had its own unique dialects.) Highly sophisticated literature, such as poetry, also existed in Arabic by that time.

THE PROPHET MUHAMMAD

It was in this environment that Muhammad was born in 570 in Mecca. He belonged to the Hashim clan of the Quraysh tribe. This clan, although not as rich as some other clans in Mecca, performed the important religious role of providing visiting pilgrims to the Ka'ba with water. Muhammad's father, Abd Allah, was the son of the clan chief, Abd al-Muttalib. Muhammad's mother was Amina. Abd Allah, like many Meccans, was involved in trade and it was on one of his trips north that he died while Amina was pregnant with Muhammad.

Amina died when Muhammad was only six years old. Abd al-Muttalib, Muhammad's grandfather, cared for the young orphan after Amina's death but he also died soon after. By the age of eight, Muhammad had lost his father, mother and grandfather. Finally, Muhammad was taken in by his uncle, Abu Talib, where he became part of the family. The large family was not well off, so Muhammad contributed to the family's welfare by occasionally working as a shepherd. He became known for his hard work and honesty. In his early twenties, this fame led to his being taken on by a wealthy widowed Meccan businesswoman named Khadija.

Muhammad worked hard for Khadija as a merchant in the caravan trade. Impressed by his integrity and honesty, she eventually proposed marriage to the young man. Although Khadija was somewhat older than Muhammad, he accepted and they were married for 25 years until Khadija's death. Muhammad took no other wife before Khadija's death. Together, they had two sons and four daughters. All of Muhammad's children, except his daughter Fatima, died before Muhammad's own death in 632.

For many years, Muhammad was simply a hard-working, respected member of the Meccan community. His reputation for honesty and truthfulness led the Meccans to use the titles 'The Trustworthy' and 'The Truthful' when referring to him. Because of his integrity and ability in peacemaking, he was often approached by Meccans to arbitrate in their disputes.

Muhammad had a predisposition to reflection and meditation.

Perhaps this was the result of his early childhood experiences of working as a shepherd and spending long hours in the barren country around Mecca. Like some other Meccans, Muhammad shunned the worshipping of idols. When he was in his thirties, he began to spend time alone, away from Mecca. He would retreat to a cave called Hira, just outside the town, where he would think and reflect.

One day, at the age of 40, when Muhammad had retired to Hira as usual, he had the startling experience of hearing a voice. The voice said: 'Read.' Muhammad replied, 'I cannot read.' The voice again commanded him to read. Muhammad repeated his reply. The third time, the voice recited the following words in Arabic which are the first revelations to Muhammad:

> Read in the name of thy Lord, who has created—created Man out of a germ-cell! Read—for thy Lord is the Most Bountiful One who has taught [Man] by the pen—taught Man what he did not know! (Qur'an 96:1–5)

Profoundly disturbed and frightened, the trembling Muhammad hurried home and sought the comfort of his wife. Khadija calmed him by saying that he was a kind man who did good deeds for his people and that he had nothing to fear. Khadija decided to take Muhammad to visit her cousin, Waraqa, an old, blind convert to Christianity, who could read the Scriptures. When Muhammad explained what had happened to him, Waraqa reassured him that his experience was similar to the experiences of earlier biblical prophets. He explained that Muhammad, too, was a prophet. Gradually, as Muhammad experienced more of these moments or 'revelations', his fear and uncertainty disappeared.

Khadija became the first person to believe in Prophet Muhammad and accept his message. She played a crucial role in supporting the Prophet and remained his most important defender until her death. Other early believers included his children, his cousin Ali who later became his son-in-law, and his close friend, Abu Bakr. For the first three years of Muhammad's prophetic life, he taught only his very close relatives and friends, explaining to them about the idea of one God and the need for social and economic justice in the Meccan community. These two teachings fundamentally challenged the life led by most Meccans. The idea of one God contradicted their belief in the existence of the many gods the Meccans worshipped, requiring them to abandon them as false idols, something the tradition-bound people of Mecca and the surrounding areas were not prepared to do. Furthermore, the idea of social and economic justice meant that the rich Meccans were now responsible for assisting the poor, needy and disadvantaged in the community.

Muhammad's claim to prophethood was met with hostility by the powerful clans and individuals in Mecca who resented the implications of the new message that Muhammad was proclaiming. Initially the opposition was mild, but it grew in strength as the Prophet began to attract more and more converts. It was only natural that his message appealed particularly to the disadvantaged, and it was these followers—without strong clan protection—who bore the greater brunt of persecution. Slaves who followed the Prophet were often severely punished and tortured, and some were even killed by their masters. Sumayya, an early convert woman, for example, was tortured to death. She is regarded as the first martyr of Islam.

As the persecution of his followers increased, the Prophet instructed some of them to leave Mecca for the neighbouring Christian kingdom of Abyssinia. A large number secretly stole away and gained the protection of the Christian king. Despite the Meccans' efforts to bring these Muslims back to Mecca, the king refused, and granted them protection and freedom to practise their new religion without any constraints. Many remained there for years.

While some of his followers had taken refuge in Abyssinia, the Prophet continued preaching in Mecca, but his hopes of further conversions vanished when he himself began to experience persecution. Although not a Muslim, Muhammad's uncle, Abu Talib, protected Muhammad from the townspeople until his own death in 619. With the death of the Prophet's most important supporter, his wife Khadija, also in 619, Muhammad lost his main sources of protection in Mecca and found himself in a precarious situation. Many of his followers in Mecca were undergoing similar suffering and persecution at the hands of their relatives.

Muhammad began to visit other tribes, clans and towns around Mecca in the hope of gaining converts, but he met with little success. His frustration increased. Yet when all seemed lost, Muhammad experienced a sudden reversal of fortune. In 620, several influential people from the town of Yathrib, some 400 kilometres to the north of Mecca, met with Muhammad and converted to Islam. In Yathrib (which later came to be known as Medina) there were two main pagan Arab tribes and three

Jewish tribes. Yathrib's peace was unsettled by a civil war between the two pagan Arab tribes, the Aws and the Khazraj. The new converts, who themselves came from the Aws and the Khazraj, hoped that the Prophet could help to arbitrate between the warring tribes, and promised him support if he decided to leave Mecca and move to Yathrib. Fortunately for the Prophet, upon their return, the new converts managed to convert a large number of people in Yathrib. With this success, the Prophet called upon his persecuted followers in Mecca to move to Yathrib (hereafter referred to as Medina) and many answered his call. They left behind their property, belongings, even their families, on secretly fleeing Mecca. In 622 the Prophet himself finally left Mecca when the townspeople threatened his life.

In contrast to Mecca, the Prophet quickly achieved success in Medina and, except for the Jewish tribes, the vast majority of the population converted to Islam within a short period of time. One of Prophet Muhammad's first actions was to secure an agreement between the Muslims and the Jews to assist each other in defending the town from outside aggression, particularly important in light of the Meccans' desire to destroy the Prophet and his message. The migration of the Prophet, known as *hijra*, in 622 and the establishment of the Muslim community at Medina marks the beginning of the Islamic calendar.

From conflict to confrontation

Medina was located strategically close to the caravan routes that passed through Mecca and this served as a powerful leverage tool for Muslims. Skirmishes began to occur between the Muslims and the Meccans. Finally, a major military conflict took place over the issue of the caravan trade. In 624, an army of 1000 Meccans led by their chiefs pitched a battle against the militarily weaker Muslim army of 313. The battle, held at Badr near Medina, was an extraordinary feat in which the Meccans were defeated and 70 of them killed, thus becoming perhaps the most significant victory for Muslims against their Meccan opponents. In this battle, family members fought against each other: father against son, brother against brother, uncle against nephew. The defeat of the Meccans dealt a massive blow to their morale, but they regrouped and carried out a revenge attack the following year. This translated into a military defeat for the Muslims, but the Meccans were unable to capitalise on their win and capture Medina itself.

A series of skirmishes continued between the two sides. In the fifth year of hijra, the Meccans gained the support of a number of other tribes for a siege of Medina. The Meccans brought 10 000 fighters to Medina and besieged it. However, the Muslims managed to dig a trench around the vulnerable parts of the town to prevent the enemy from entering. The strategy succeeded. Frustrated, many fighters left the siege and the Meccans had to return without achieving either of their objectives: the destruction of Medina and Islam *once and for all*.

This siege, also known as the Battle of Khandaq, and the Meccans' defeat led tribes from around Medina who until then had been 'sitting on the fence' to shift their allegiance to the Muslims. Many converted to Islam, while others made peace with the Muslims. Muslim influence began to increase significantly, while the Meccans' influence was gradually on the decline.

Nevertheless, the Meccans continued with their efforts to destroy the Prophet and the Muslims.

Prophet Muhammad's return to Mecca

Finally, eight years after fleeing Mecca, the Prophet led an army of 10 000 and entered the town without any bloodshed. The Meccans simply were unable to resist such a well-armed force. The Prophet had given strict orders to Muslims not to engage in any fighting except in self-defence. Before entering Mecca, he also announced to the Meccans that those who remained indoors would not be harmed. Most Meccans decided to avoid any clash with the Muslims and thus bloodshed was avoided. One of the first things the Prophet did when he entered Mecca was to go to Ka'ba and destroy all the idols placed there. The Ka'ba was once again devoted solely to the worship of one God, Allah.

The Prophet brought together in a meeting place those Meccans who for years had sought the destruction of Islam and persecuted the Muslims. He informed that there would be no revenge against them and declared a general amnesty. The Meccans had not expected such generous treatment. The Prophet had the power to do whatever he wanted to them. He could have wreaked havoc in the town. It was, perhaps, this generosity and forgiveness on the part of the Prophet that led the vast majority of Meccans to embrace the new religion within a short period of time.

Having gained control of Mecca, the Prophet returned to Medina where he stayed until his death two years later in 632. At his passing, the greater part of Arabia had accepted Islam, or had at least concluded peace treaties with the Prophet. An indication of his success by this time is that just before his death, he made a pilgrimage to Mecca where he was joined by 100 000 Muslims from all over Arabia.

The death of the Prophet

When the Prophet died in 632, the community was left without any clear instructions as to who would succeed as political leader of the Muslims, by this time the most powerful force in Arabia. Upon the Prophet's death, the Medinan Muslims attempted to appoint a leader from among themselves. The Meccan Muslims (many of whom were also living in Medina) wanted to appoint one from among their own. After a heated debate, it was decided that the Prophet's closest friend and one of the earliest converts, Abu Bakr, was to lead the Muslim community. Of the Prophet's family, only his daughter, Fatima, remained alive. The closest male relative to the Prophet was his cousin and son-in-law, Fatima's husband, Ali, who was much younger than Abu Bakr. Some in the community, particularly the family of the Prophet led by Ali, felt that they should have been consulted and given priority in the appointment of a successor to the Prophet.

Abu Bakr remained as leader, or caliph, for two years. During this time he faced a number of challenges, including armed rebellion from Arab tribes who refused to recognise him as the legitimate successor to the Prophet, and many of whom reverted back to their previous religious beliefs. Much of Arabia rebelled against Medina, leaving only Medina, Mecca and the surrounding areas under the control of Abu Bakr. However, Abu Bakr managed to defeat the rebels and to bring much of Arabia once again under Medina's control.

THE SPREAD OF ISLAM

The emergence of Islam in Arabia, the Prophet's success in converting much of Arabia to Islam, and Abu Bakr's quelling of the rebellion of the Arab tribes, were important events not lost on the two powerful empires to the north and northeast of Arabia: the Christian Byzantines and the largely Zoroastrian Sassanids. Both saw the success of the Muslims as a significant threat. Both empires had control of client tribes to the north and northeast of Arabia, and they attempted to use those tribes to challenge the growing power of the Muslims. The tension between Muslims and the two neighbouring empires began to simmer. Abu Bakr decided to face the new threat coming from outside Arabia head-on. He directed small armies towards both the Byzantines and the Sassanids. In the initial clashes, Muslims overpowered their enemies even though their enemies were more resourceful, and better organised and equipped. The initial successes led to further advances against the two empires by Abu Bakr and his successor, Umar. Within a short period of time, the Muslim armies had brought about the collapse of the Sassanid empire and of a large part of the Byzantine empire.

The approach Abu Bakr adopted in this war against the Byzantines and Sassanids is expressed in his famous instruction to his generals:

> Do not betray, or misappropriate any part of the booty. Do not practise treachery or mutilation. Do not kill a child, an old

man, or a woman. Do not destroy or burn palm trees. Do not cut down fruit trees. Do not slaughter a sheep or a cow or a camel, except for food. You will meet people who have set themselves apart in monasteries. Leave them to accomplish the purpose for which they have done this.[1]

Within only one hundred years of the Prophet's death, Muslim political rule had spread westward towards what is today Spain as well as West Africa, and eastward towards the borders of China, India and Central Asia. When Muslims 'conquered' these regions, they allowed the inhabitants to remain faithful to their own religions. Jewish communities remained Jewish; Christians remained Christian. What had changed for these inhabitants was that the empires which used to rule over them (Byzantines and Sassanids) were now replaced by Arab-Muslims. The taxes they used to pay to these empires now went to the Arab-Muslims. Given that the Muslim tax was set at a relatively low rate, in many cases the changeover seemed positive from the perspective of the inhabitants. It took more than 200 years for the people of these regions to convert to Islam.

The rapid expansion of Muslim power throughout the then known world led to the emergence of what we may call Islamic civilisation. Initially, power remained under the central control of a caliph based in Medina. Later the seat of power moved to Damascus, and much later to Baghdad. From the tenth century CE, however, centralised and unified Muslim power no longer existed. Over the next 1000 years many great empires and king-doms emerged and disappeared in what we call today the world of Islam.

Chronology of Political Events

610 The first revelation in the cave at Mt. Hira. The Prophet Muhammad is commissioned as the Messenger of God

615 Persecution of the Muslims by the Quraysh. A party of Muslims leaves for Abyssinia

621 Pledge at Aqaba (with Muslim converts from Yathrib)

622 The Prophet and the Muslims migrate to Yathrib

624 Battle of Badr

625 Battle of Uhud

627 Battle of the Trench (Khandaq)

630 Muslims conquer Mecca

632 Death of the Prophet. Election of Abu Bakr as the Caliph

634 Death of Abu Bakr; Umar becomes the Caliph

635 Muslim conquest of Damascus

636 Muslim conquest of Madain (Ctesiphon)

637 Muslim conquest of Syria. Fall of Jerusalem

642 Muslim conquest of Egypt

643 Muslim conquest of parts of Central Asia

644 Death of Umar. Uthman becomes the Caliph

656 Death of Uthman. Ali becomes the Caliph. Battle of the Camel

661 Death of Ali. Mu'awiya becomes the sole Caliph

670 Muslim advance in North Africa

674 Muslims cross the Oxus

680 Death of Mu'awiya. Accession of Yazid. Tragedy of Karbala and martyrdom of Husayn

712 Muslims advance in Spain, Sind and Transoxiana

732 The Battle of Tours in France

750 End of the Umayyads. The beginning of Abbasids

756 Abd al-Rahman founds the Umayyad state in Spain

763 Foundation of Baghdad

969 The Fatimids conquer Egypt

1019 Conquest of the Punjab by Mahmud Ghaznavi

1091 The Normans conquer the island of Sicily; end of the Muslim rule there

1095 The first crusade

1099 The Crusaders capture Jerusalem

1171 Salah al-Din (Saladin) founds the Ayyubid dynasty in Egypt

1187 Salah al-Din wrests Jerusalem from the Christians

1194 Occupation of Delhi by the Muslims

1258 The Mongols sack Baghdad. End of the Abbasid rule

1273 Death of Jalaluddin Rumi

1453 Capture of Constantinople by the Turks

1501 Isamil I establishes the Safavid dynasty in Persia, and the Twelve-Imam Shi'ism becomes the state religion

1526 The Battle of Panipat in India, and the Mughal conquest; Babur makes his capital at Delhi and Agra

1529 Unsuccessful Ottoman siege of Vienna

1550 Islam spreads to Java, the Moluccas, and Borneo

1571 The Ottomans are defeated at the naval Battle of Lepanto, and their dominance in the Mediterranean is brought to a close

1605 Death of the Mughal emperor Akbar

1631 Death of Mumtaz Mahal, wife of Mughal Emperor Shah Jahan and the lady of Taj Mahal, Agra

1683 Second Ottoman siege of Vienna and retreat

1804 Othman Dan Fodio established Islamic State of Sokoto

1827 Malaya became a preserve of the British

1828 Russia declared war against Turkey

1830 French forces landed near Algiers and occupied Algeria

1857 British captured Delhi and eliminated Mughal rule in India after 332 years. Last Mughal Emperor Bahadur Shah Zafar was exiled to Rangoon in Burma

1859 Imam Shamil laid down arms before Russian forces and the Islamic State of Daghestan became a Russian province

1878 Turkey handed over Cyprus to Britain

1881 France invaded Tunisia

1881 Muhammad Ahmad declared himself Mahdi in northern Sudan

1882 Egypt came under British military occupation

1885 Death of Mahdi of Sudan five months after the occupation of Khartum

1895 Mirza Ghulam Ahmad of Qadian claimed prophethood

1901 Ibn Saud (Abd al-Aziz) captures Riyadh

1901 French forces occupy Morocco

1907 The beginning of the Young Turks movement in Turkey

1912 The beginning of the Muhammadiyya reform movement in Indonesia

1914 World War I

1916 Arab revolt against Ottoman (Turkish) rule. Lawrence of Arabia leads attacks on the Hijaz Railway

1918 World War I ends

1918 Syria and Damascus become a French protectorate

1924 The Ottoman Turkish Caliphate is abolished

1924 King Abd al-Aziz conquers Mecca and Medina, which leads to the unification of the Kingdoms of Najd and Hijaz

1925 Reza Khan seizes the government in Persia and establishes the Pahlavi dynasty

1928 Turkey is declared a secular state

1928 Hasan al-Banna founds the Muslim Brotherhood in Egypt

1932 Iraq granted independence by the League of Nations

1935 Iran becomes the official name of Persia

1936 Increased Jewish immigration provokes widespread Arab–Jewish fighting in Palestine

1939 World War II

1943 Lebanon becomes independent from France

1945 End of World War II

1946 Jordan and Syria become independent from Britain and France respectively

1947 Creation of Pakistan

1948 Creation of state of Israel. Arab armies suffer defeat in war with Israel. Displacement of hundreds of thousands of Palestinians from British-mandated Palestine

1949 Hasan al-Banna, leader of the Muslim Brotherhood, is assassinated

1951 Libya becomes independent

1952 King Faruq of Egypt forced to abdicate

1953 Death of King Abd al-Aziz (Ibn Saud) of Saudi Arabia

1956 Morocco becomes independent

1956 Tunisia becomes independent

1957 The Bey of Tunisia is deposed, and Bourguiba becomes president

1962 Algeria becomes independent

1965 Malcom X is assassinated

1967 The Arab–Israeli war (known as the 'six-day war')

1968 The enlargement of the Haram in Mecca is completed

1969 King Idris of Libya is ousted by a coup led by Colonel Qaddafi

1973 King Zahir Shah of Afghanistan is overthrown

1975 Death of Elijah Mohammad, leader of Nation of Islam among African Americans in North America

1975 Wallace Warith Deen Mohammad assumes leadership of Nation of Islam and shifts movement toward Islamic Orthodoxy, renaming it American Muslim Mission. Lebanese civil war begins

1979 The Shah leaves Iran on January 15, thus bringing the Pahlavi dynasty to an end. Iranian Islamic revolution under the leadership of Ayatollah Khomeini

1980 Beginning of the Iran–Iraq war

1982 Israel invades Lebanon

1987 The first Palestinian Intifada (uprising) against Israeli occupation

1989 Iran–Iraq war comes to an end with much loss of life

1990 Military annexation of Kuwait by Iraq

1991 An international coalition led by the United States go to war against Iraq (Gulf War) and drive Iraq out of Kuwait

2000 Second Intifada begins in Palestine
2001 Attacks on New York and Washington (September 11)
and the subsequent American attack on Afghanistan

adapted from the Website:
http://www.usc.edu/dept/MSA/history/chronology/index.html

Islamic civilisation

Within one hundred years or so of the death of the Prophet,
Muslims acquired control of the Middle East, North Africa,
West Asia, Central Asia and South Asia up to the borders of
modern India, as well as parts of Europe. In the process, the
Islamic empire (or caliphate) brought together under one banner
large numbers of Christian, Jewish, Buddhist, Hindu, Zoroastrian
and pagan communities. It also managed to bring their intellectual traditions, scientific and philosophical works, libraries,
scholars and translators together to initiate what came to be
known as one of the most ambitious 'knowledge projects' in the
pre-modern period.

The caliph (equivalent to an emperor), his court and other
lesser rulers based in Damascus, Baghdad, Cairo and Cordova
financed massive projects of collecting and purchasing manu-
scripts from the Greeks, Byzantines, Persians and Indians, among
others. The Muslim rulers established translation centres where
scholars from Christian, Jewish and other backgrounds were
employed to translate and expand on the knowledge of the
Greeks, Romans, Persians and Indians, and material from

whatever sources they could find. Initially, translators were mostly non-Muslim scholars, but Muslims soon joined the growing ranks of the intellectual elite.

Libraries and universities were established in all major cities of the empire. Scholars were encouraged to engage in research and were generously rewarded. Scientific achievements were translated into practical solutions, such as dams, water purification and the provision of running water, bridges, roads, new weapons, observatories, agriculture, administrative systems, mining and manufacturing. All of this took place from the eighth century CE onwards, at a time when major parts of Europe were backward and poor.

CONTRIBUTIONS TO SCIENCE BY ISLAMIC CIVILISATION

In the early stages of Islamic history—from around 700 to 800 CE—the main scientific and philosophical activity was the translation of works from Greek, Syriac, Persian and Sanskrit into Arabic, the *lingua franca* of the Islamic civilisation. The language of high culture, Arabic was the main tongue in which scholars from Muslim, Christian, Jewish and other backgrounds wrote their works. Translations were made of the medical, astronomical, mathematical, pharmacological, botanical, literary, historical and philosophical works of Greeks, Romans, Egyptians, Persians and Indians.

The following are some of the intellectual achievements made by scholars of the Islamic civilisation.

Mathematics

- Adaptation and development of Sanskrit numerals, which later came to be known in Europe as Arabic numerals, the number system we use today.
- Development of the decimal system.
- Contributions to geometry, algebra and trigonometry.
- Development of plane and solid geometry.
- Development of algebraic equations up to the third degree and systematisation of the solution of quadratic equations. Interestingly, the English word 'algebra' is derived from Arabic, from the title of a book on algebra—*al-Jabr wa al-Muqabala*—written by the famous Muslim mathematician al-Khwarizmi (d. ca 850).

Astronomy

- Synthesis of the astronomical works of Greeks, Indians and Babylonians.
- Setting up of observatories as scientific institutions, including in places such as Maraghah and Samarqand.
- Development of observational instruments such as the astrolabe, the sextant and the quadrant.
- New approaches to the calculation of the movements of the planets.

Physics

- New research on light by figures such as Ibn al-Haytham (d. 1040) (known in Latin as Alhazen), who carried out research on refraction and reflection. He arrived at the solution to what is known today as 'Alhazen's Problem'.

- Contribution to the study of motion, and criticisms of the Aristotelian theory of motion.

Chemistry

- Establishment of laboratories.
- Division of substances into plant, mineral or animal.
- Separation of alchemy from chemistry, and providing the foundation for the development of chemistry.

Medicine

- Discovering new diseases and their treatments such as small pox.
- Giving a detailed account of the anatomy of the bladder.
- Describing operations to remove renal stones or to break them.
- Writing of major original works on medicine, such as that of al-Razi (d. 930) (known as Rhazes) and Ibn Sina (d. 1037) (known as Avicenna). Ibn Sina's famous book *The Canon* was used as a medical textbook in the West for 700 years.
- Islamic Spain's al-Zahrawi (d. 1013), among other Muslim surgeons, performed surgery under inhalation anaesthesia with the use of narcotic-soaked sponges which were placed over the face.

Geography

- Several geographers at the House of Knowledge, Baghdad, compiled the first atlas of the world which included a map of the Sea of Java, probably the first map bearing an outline of northern Australia.
- Maps drawn of the world, without which Christopher Columbus probably would not have been able to cross the Atlantic.

Geology

- Research on rocks, including their formation, and on sedimentation, mountains and oceans.

Music

- Explaining the phenomenon of sound, intervals and composition.
- Providing a lute fretting that combined the basic diatonic arrangement of Pythagorean intervals with additional frets suited for playing two newly introduced neutral, or microtonal, intervals.

The contributions of the Islamic civilisation to science and other areas were translated from Arabic into Latin from around the eleventh century onwards. The achievements of the Islamic civilisation provided the foundations for the European Renaissance and Western science. For approximately 700 years—until the fourteenth century—the Islamic civilisation contributed greatly to world history and civilisation and was arguably the most important factor in facilitating subsequent scientific achievements.

Rasheeda Cooper
Being a Muslim musician

I learnt to play the piano when I was young. I now teach piano and facilitate a music and movement class for parents, babies and toddlers. In recent years, I have been learning to play the tabla, which is a classical Indian instrument consisting of a pair of drums. By learning tabla I feel part of the Muslim Moghul tradition under whose patronage this instrument developed. Many of the rhythms have been passed down through Muslim families over many centuries. I enjoy playing with friends informally after dinner, as well as performing at functions and events such as weddings and Muslim festivals. Music leads me to worship God, who created a universe of beauty and order, and who is the Source and Inspiration of all our creativity.

Chapter 3

*I*SLAMIC WORLD VIEW

Like other great religious traditions, such as Judaism and Christianity, Islam is fundamentally concerned with the ultimate questions of life. Who are we? Where do we come from? How should we live our life? Where will we end up? Islam's answers to these essential questions reveal that there is much in common between Islam, Christianity and Judaism. From a Muslim perspective, this similarity is not accidental; it is because all three religious traditions emanate from the same source: God. Their basic message is essentially the same, and the answers they give to the fundamental questions in life are similar. Emphasising that the God of Muhammad and Muslims is the same God as the God of the Jews and Christians, the Qur'an, the Holy Scripture of Muslims, says:

> . . . [O Muslims] say [to the Jews and Christians]: 'We believe in the Revelation which has come down to us and in that which

came down to you; our God and your God is One; and it is to Him we bow in submission.' (Qur'an 29:46)

Similarly, the Qur'an emphasises that all prophets before Muhammad were sent by God and that Muhammad is not unique among them. In fact, a Muslim must believe in *all* prophets who came before Muhammad. For instance, if a Muslim says, 'I don't believe in Moses, Jesus, Jacob or Isaac', the person cannot be a Muslim. As for Jesus, a Muslim believes that he is one of the greatest prophets but not the son of God. Emphasising that all prophets before Muhammad came also from God, the Qur'an says:

We have sent thee [O Muhammad] Revelation as We sent it to Noah and the Messengers after him. We sent Revelation to Abraham, Ishmael, Isaac, Jacob and the tribes, to Jesus, Job, Jonah, Aaron, and Solomon, and to David We gave the Psalms. Of some apostles We have already told thee the story; of others We have not; And to Moses God spoke direct. (Qur'an 4:163–4)

When Australians of Jewish or Christian backgrounds read the Qur'an, they will find that many of the ideas in the Bible are also found in the Qur'an. The Qur'an also contains many stories relating to biblical prophets. Indeed, some of the chapters of the Qur'an are named after biblical figures such as Abraham, Jonah, Joseph and Mary. It is no wonder, then, that there is so much similarity between Islam, Christianity and Judaism in terms of their fundamental beliefs.

Beliefs about the creation of the universe

Muslims believe that this universe and everything within it was 'created' by a power other than itself: God. Everything in the universe 'submits' to God, including all of nature, the galaxies, stars, planets and black holes. While time itself began when the universe was created, Islam does not specify how long ago this occurred, or exactly how it happened. The Qur'an does not state that everything was brought into being the way it is now; it is completely open to the idea that the universe took eons to create. Thus, there is no inherent contradiction between the idea of God creating the universe, and the possibility of it evolving over billions of years. Islam is not so much concerned with how the process of creation happened, but rather with the idea that it is God who brought it into being.

Thus, in whatever form the universe and everything in it 'evolved' and however many billions of years it took to reach the stage in which we see them, it is still God's creation: God is the Creator and Sustainer of the Universe. Muslims believe that God, having created the universe, did not leave it to run on its own. For Muslims, God has His own way of maintaining and sustaining the creative process. Exactly how He does this—for example, through natural laws—does not affect the religious faith of Muslims. Instead, they are more interested in the idea that everything comes from God and in the end will return to Him. This grand scheme of creation was not without purpose, as the Qur'an states that everything in the universe has been created for a reason. From the smallest bacterium to galaxies, everything has its place and is connected with everything else.

While some Australian Muslims still reject the theories of evolution, many educated Muslims (both young and old) will be comfortable with the view presented above. The polarised nature of the debate on evolution and creation in certain quarters in Christian circles is not a characteristic of the debate among Muslims in Australia.

BELIEFS ABOUT THE CREATION OF HUMAN BEINGS

Within this broad scheme of creation, Muslims believe that at a certain point in time, God brought to life the first human being. Whether this took thousands of years or not, the important idea to a Muslim is that it is God who brought about our design and creation. The Qur'an narrates the story of the creation of the human being in a number of places. In fact, some verses of the Qur'an, such as the following, give the impression that it may have taken a very long time for humans to emerge as we exist today: 'It is He that has created you in diverse stages.' (Qur'an 71:14)

The Qur'an narrates the creation of the first human being, Adam, and his companion, Eve (Hawwa). When God wanted to create the first human being, the Qur'an narrates that God said to the angels:

'I will create a vicegerent on earth.' They [angels] said: 'Wilt Thou place therein one who will make mischief therein and shed blood? Whilst we do celebrate Thy praises and glorify

Thy holy name?' He said: 'I know what ye know not.' (Qur'an 2:30)

Once created, God commanded the angels to prostrate to this human being as a sign of respect. All except Satan (Iblis), the symbolic figure representing evil, obeyed. For his disobedience, God banished him from the heavens but he was given leave from punishment until the Day of Judgment. Adam and Eve were then asked to remain in the 'Garden'. God tested them by commanding them not to eat from a particular tree. However, Satan took his revenge for his banishment by encouraging Adam and Eve to eat from that tree. Both Adam and Eve failed the first test; they both ate from the forbidden tree. Muslims believe that Adam and Eve were 'moved out' of the Garden because both disobeyed a command of God, and also that the Garden was not meant to be the permanent place for them to live. From the Garden, they were moved to the world in which they had to face all the difficulties and challenges of life.

Muslims do not believe in the concept of 'original sin' or that the sin committed by Adam and Eve is somehow 'transferred' to their descendants. Nor do they believe that Eve was somehow responsible for committing the sin; in the story in the Qur'an, it is both Adam and Eve who committed it.

In relating the story of Adam and Eve, the Qur'an describes their mutual partnership as the first parents. They form the original nucleus, and through them all human beings belong to one family. The Qur'an says:

O humankind! Be conscious of your Sustainer, who has created you out of one living entity, and out of it created its mate, and out of the two spread abroad a multitude of men and women. (Qur'an 4:1)

Because all human beings came from the same parents, Adam and Eve, everyone is considered equal before God in Islam. While in theory, no Muslim should claim that they are better than another based for any reason, whether on race, language, culture, ethnicity, lineage, wealth, sex or beauty, the practice may vary from culture to culture among Muslims.

When God created Adam and Eve, He also provided them with guidance and support. He taught them that they were created by God and should submit to His will. He provided them with instructions on how to be conscious of God, to function as human beings and to relate to each other in society. Muslims believe that Adam represents not only the first human being, but also the first prophet, and it was his duty to pass on God's teachings to his descendants.

According to the Qur'an, human beings are created free from sin. All have the capacity to do good and shun evil. This means that every human being starts life with a totally clean slate and develops according to the upbringing of his or her parents and the environment in which he or she is placed, thus growing up as a Christian, Jew, Muslim or any other. When a person reaches maturity, it becomes their duty to reflect upon the choices they make and to select the right course of action. Whenever God's message reaches a person, they have the duty to decide whether to follow it or not. Life in this world is a test: those who follow God's guidance are considered successful, and those who do not will face their Lord on the Day of Judgment and will be answerable for the choices they made in their life. God gave each human being the ability to make these choices.

BELIEFS ABOUT THE PURPOSE OF LIFE

Muslims believe that God has endowed human beings with the faculty of reason. This gives human beings the ability to choose whether they wish to follow the guidelines that God has provided them through His prophets or not. According to the Qur'an, if a person chooses to believe in God and to follow His instructions, they will have made the right choice and be considered successful. This is not measured in terms of material gain, such as fortune or fame, but rather by spiritual gain. Real success lies in following God's guidance and helping others in the path as well. All of this depends, of course, on individual ability. For example, some possess more purpose means than others and therefore have an extra responsibility to provide for those who have less. Ultimately, the purpose of life here on earth is for each to fulfil his or her individual potential to the fullest, as well as to contribute to the well-being of others. In this way, we live up to our human nature, which, according to the Qur'an, is to serve God and submit to His will.

BELIEFS ABOUT LIFE AFTER DEATH

Islam teaches that death is inevitable. According to Muslim belief, when the time of death comes, there is no escape from it. The Angel of Death, who is responsible for death, will come and 'remove' one's soul at the appointed time. After death, another life begins: life in the 'grave'. We do not know how this life is.

Islam teaches that after death, at a particular time, there will be a momentous occasion called the Day of Judgment. On this day, all human beings will be brought to life again and God will present to each person a record of how they conducted their lives. Each person will be judged according to the choices they made, how they behaved, the contributions they offered and whether they fulfilled their individual capacity. If a person is judged successful, the reward is blissful everlasting life. If judged unsuccessful, the person will be committed to a life that is truly awful.

Chapter 4

ESSENTIAL BELIEFS
AND PRACTICES

How does a person become a Muslim? The answer to this question is very simple, but putting it into practice takes a lifetime. Those who are born into a Muslim family grow up as Muslims, while others convert to Islam. In Australia, converts come from a variety of ethnic, religious and cultural backgrounds. To become a Muslim, a person makes a special vow by reciting what is called the *shahada*, which is: 'There is no god but God and Muhammad is the Messenger of God' (*La ilaha illa Allah, Muhammad rasul Allah*). By pronouncing this formula and adopting it as a system of belief, a person immediately becomes a Muslim; there are no other rituals for accepting Islam. However, this is just the entry level, and once a person becomes a Muslim, there are some beliefs and practices that he or she needs to accept and follow.

ESSENTIAL BELIEFS

Muslims, including those in Australia, subscribe to the following beliefs.

Belief in one God

The first and foremost belief of a Muslim is to acknowledge the one God who is the Creator and Sustainer of all that exists. In Arabic, the word for God is 'Allah', and often Muslims prefer to use this name.

Muslims believe there is only one God, even if He is referred to by different names. This belief in one God is the most fundamental belief in Islam, and the rest of the religion is built upon it. The Qur'an says:

> Say [O Muhammad to people] that He is One God; Allah, the Eternal Absolute. He neither gives birth nor was He ever begotten, and there is nothing equal to Him. (Qur'an 112:1–4)

Believing in one God means acknowledging that it is to Him alone that everyone and everything submits, and that it is through Him alone that true guidance comes.

A Muslim believes that although God is One, He has many 'beautiful names' of which the Qur'an mentions several, such as Merciful, Compassionate, Forgiving, Just and Creator. Islam teaches that:

- God is not male or female; He has no gender. When we use terms like 'He' to refer to God, it is merely because we do not have an appropriate word to refer to Him.

- No one can imagine how God 'looks', and therefore cannot make any representation of God; there is nothing like God in the universe at all.
- God has no beginning or end. It is God who created time. Time begins with the creation of the universe, and thus God is 'outside' time and space.
- Every human being has access to God and everyone can speak directly to God. Because God knows everything that is happening in the universe, He hears when we speak to Him through our prayers. No one needs an intermediary between God and him or her. According to the Qur'an, God is 'closer' to each person than one's jugular vein.

Belief in the prophets

From Adam the first prophet, to Muhammad the last, the institution of prophethood has continued throughout human history. Muslims believe that God has sent prophets and messengers to all the peoples of the earth. From the Aboriginal people of ancient lands to the modern societies of the world, no single community has remained without guidance. The Qur'an only mentions the names of 25 prophetic figures; however, according to tradition, God has sent over 100 000 prophets before Muhammad, although we do not know the histories or details of the vast majority of them.

Muslims believe that these prophets all came with essentially the same message: that we have a duty to recognise the Creator and submit to His will. The idea of submission to God is an essential element of all revelations, although different messengers also brought different social teachings depending on the needs and requirements of the times in which they lived. This means that differences in religious traditions can be traced to local factors such as the environment, context, culture, time-period and so on.

Based on this, Muslims believe that the Prophet Muhammad did not bring a new religion; in fact, Islam (which literally means 'submission') was the religion of all the prophets of God. In the Qur'an, Abraham and Noah are referred to as Muslims, as are David, Jacob, Joseph, Jesus and Muhammad. A Muslim is simply one who submits to God, and so all prophets in this sense were Muslim.

Belief in the Scriptures

The third belief is that not only did God send messengers and prophets, but that at times God provided certain instructions (revelations) which took shape in different forms, including the written Scriptures. The Qur'an mentions a number of these Scriptures. Muslims believe that God revealed the Torah (Tawrah) and the Gospel (Injil), among others, but that the Qur'an is the final Scripture from God. For a Muslim, the Qur'an is literally the word of God, in Arabic.

Belief in angels

The fourth belief is that God created special beings called angels. Even though we do not know what these beings are like, Muslims believe that they exist and have been given certain functions and duties to fulfil. Only some angels are mentioned in the Qur'an, such as Jibril (Gabriel), whose job is to carry messages of divine guidance to the prophets, but there are probably billions of them. Muslims believe that each angel has an assigned function by God and, unlike human beings, they do not have the power to disobey God.

Belief in the Day of Judgment

The fifth belief is in the Day of Judgment, when the universe as we know it will end and everyone will be held accountable for their actions in this life. Exactly when it will occur, what will happen during it, and how long it will take are all unknown.

Muslims believe that every act, word and thought of each person is recorded like a film. On the Day of Judgment, God will give each person this record of all their actions, deeds and thoughts: good and bad. It is largely on the basis of this record that God will decide who has failed the test of life in this world and who has passed. Those who failed the great test will be sent to Hell and those who passed will go to Paradise.

Islam teaches that Paradise is a place that has not been experienced by a human being, and therefore one cannot 'imagine' exactly what it will be like. There are many references to Paradise in the Qur'an and in the traditions of the Prophet. But these descriptions are based on our experiences in life lived in this world. The reality may be very different. In one of the traditions of the Prophet, he reportedly said that Paradise will be unlike anything that could ever be imagined by a human being.

Belief in God's foreknowledge and destiny

The sixth belief is that God knows everything that happens in the universe. He knows the past, present and future, although we cannot understand how. This means that good and bad things may happen for a reason that is unclear to us. Thus, patience in the face of adversity is expected of a Muslim. Islam teaches that:

- God's foreknowledge of what will happen does not force a person to act in a particular way.
- Each person has the ability to make choices in life: to do or not to do a particular thing, or to follow or not to follow a particular religion, for instance.
- Each person should make every possible effort to achieve whatever objectives they set for themselves.

FUNDAMENTAL PRACTICES

In addition to the six core beliefs, there are a number of practices that a Muslim is required to perform. Following on from the shahada (making a declaration that there is no god but God and that Muhammad is the Messenger of God), the other four fundamental practices—sometimes referred to as the 'pillars' of Islam—are considered compulsory for every Muslim who can fulfil them. If any person neglects to carry them out, he or she is considered to have breached their contract with God.

Daily prayers (salat)

The first practice is to perform five daily prayers, known as salat in Arabic. Each day is divided up into five periods during which the prayer has to be performed. The five daily prayers and times are: *Fajr* (between dawn and sunrise); *Zuhr* (from noon until afternoon); *Asr* (from afternoon until sunset); *Maghrib* (from sunset until about an hour later); *Isha* (from an hour or so after sunset through the rest of the night).

Just as a church bell rings out to call the faithful to church in some countries, in Muslim countries a call to prayer, or *adhan*, can be heard from the mosque five times a day. The call to prayer is in Arabic throughout the Muslim world. The meaning of adhan is as follows:

God is the greatest. God is the greatest.
God is the greatest. God is the greatest.
I declare there is no god but God.
I declare there is no god but God.
I declare Muhammad is the Messenger of God.
I declare Muhammad is the Messenger of God.
Rush to prayer. Rush to prayer.
Rush to success. Rush to success.
God is the greatest. God is the greatest.
There is no god but God.

However, in Australia, where Muslims are a minority, they may not make the call to prayer loudly because of council restrictions. A mosque is not necessarily built in a 'Muslim area'. In fact, many neighbours of mosques are non-Muslim. To avoid causing a disturbance to the neighbours, mosques attempt to keep the noise and traffic levels to a minimum.

Given that the call to prayer is made inside an Australian

mosque and is not heard outside, Muslims, even those who live close to the mosque, will have to check the prayer times (published regularly by mosques and Islamic centres) to know when the prayer is to be held. When the time for prayer comes, Muslim men from the neighbourhood will generally visit the mosque to pray there. However, because Muslims can pray in any clean place, it is not uncommon to see them praying in a park, or in a quiet corner of an unused room at work.

Before each prayer, one is expected to wash one's hands, face, arms and feet. Under certain circumstances, one may have to take a shower or a bath before praying in order to make oneself ritually clean. The Muslim must wear clean clothes that cover the body. For a man, this means covering the body at least from navel to knee, and for a woman it means the entire body except the face and hands. If the prayer is performed outside a mosque, the place has to be clean. A few places are declared unsuitable for prayer, such as toilets, rubbish dumps and other dirty places. One can pray, say, in a park, on a footpath or anywhere else that is clean.

The Muslim faces towards Mecca and commences the prayer. If there is more than one person, the prayer leader (*imam*) stands in front of the others who form rows, one behind the other. Where there are men and women, they form separate rows. The prayer involves a number of movements: standing, bowing down, prostrating, sitting, and recitation of the Qur'an and set prayers. Each prayer has its own format and one is expected to complete them as a set.

The purpose of prayer is to keep in regular touch with God and to be mindful of His presence in daily life. It also helps the believer to remember to avoid bad deeds and to ask for forgiveness for any sins that he or she may have committed. The Prophet likened the prayer to bathing in a river five times a day, so that the Muslim becomes spiritually clean.

There are other special prayer times during the Islamic calendar. Once a week, on Friday, a service is held at noon, in which Muslims gather in congregation to pray. There are also two special days (called *Eid*) that occur during the Islamic year, when Muslims gather to pray and celebrate.

As well as the obligatory prayers, Muslims are encouraged to perform voluntary prayers, which can take many different forms. At other times, Muslims may simply supplicate to God (*du'a*, in Arabic) and ask for his guidance and protection. Such supplications can be said in any language. Normally, when Muslims supplicate, they raise their hands and hold them together in front of them. When the supplication is finished, they touch their face with both hands.

An example of a du'a is as follows:

O Allah, forgive me my sins and my ignorance, my excesses in my deeds and what you know better about than I myself. O Allah, forgive me the wrongs I did lightly and seriously, and my accidental and intentional transgressions, and all that is with me.

Another type of worship is to meditatively recite the most beautiful names of God and phrases glorifying Him, or simply to recite the Qur'an. While the prayer (salat) is conducted in Arabic, just as the Prophet Muhammad instructed his followers to pray, it is very important to understand what the words and movements mean.

For an Australian practising Muslim, performing the five daily prayers is not an onerous task. At work, it is usually easy to find a few minutes during the lunch or coffee break for prayer.

Fasting (sawm)

Just as in many other religious traditions, Muslims are required to fast at certain times. Once a year, during the month of Ramadan, Muslims abstain from food, drink, smoking and sex during daylight hours from dawn to sunset.

As the Islamic calendar is a lunar one, the month of Ramadan can last for 29 or 30 days, depending on the movement of the moon. Ramadan shifts backwards through the solar year, as there are approximately 11 to 12 days less in the lunar year. This means that over the course of a lifetime, a Muslim would experience fasting during all four seasons and lengths of day.

Fasting is more than just giving up bodily pleasures, however; it is a time to develop spiritually as well. During Ramadan, Muslims are encouraged to spend much time in prayer and contemplation, remembering and helping the more disadvantaged members of the community who may not have access to food and the basic necessities of life. It is also a time for forgiveness, for making amends with others and avoiding any bad deeds or sins, in an attempt to become even closer to God. Ramadan has been compared to a training camp: if a Muslim can exert his or her utmost efforts to develop spiritually during the time when it is perhaps most difficult, then he or she will be more likely to continue with the pattern for the rest of the year.

Devout Muslims do not consider Ramadan a hardship; on the contrary, it is perhaps the most eagerly awaited period of the year. Before dawn, all the members of the family and any guests gather together to eat a meal called *suhur*. Special foods are prepared, as it is the last chance to eat and drink before fasting begins for the day. Then, at sunset, Muslims break their fast with a meal called *iftar*. This is a joyous occasion, and it is customary to visit the homes of family and friends so that iftar can be shared together. Usually, the iftar consists of dates, water, juice or soup, and fruit. This may differ from culture to culture. After iftar, the believer may then rush to pray the Maghrib prayer and then return to share dinner with family and friends. Also, during Ramadan, special prayers called *tarawih* are conducted. They are performed after the last of the five daily prayers. Many Muslim men, women and children like to attend mosques and prayer houses in order to perform tarawih. In Australia, restaurants owned by Muslims may open long into the night as friends get together to celebrate the special month.

The last ten days of Ramadan are particularly important. During this period, many devout Muslims tend to spend much time in the mosque, particularly at night. One of the nights of the last ten days is what is known in Islam as the 'Night of Power' (*laylat al-qadr*). It is a night of blessing, and Muslims endeavour to receive the blessings of this night by spending the last ten nights praying, meditating and reciting the Qur'an.

During Ramadan many Muslim countries reduce work hours to make it easier for people to function while fasting. Sometimes, particularly if Ramadan falls during summer when the days are long and fasting is more difficult, a substantial amount of work that is usually conducted during the day is shifted to the night, and in some places shops are open all night long and close about an hour before dawn. This is not the case everywhere, and Australian Muslims do not have that luxury. But no matter where Ramadan is observed, normal duties continue throughout the month, as it is not a month of cessation of work. During Ramadan, Australian Muslims go about their daily work to earn their livelihood. In some places, the only clue that it is Ramadan is that Muslim employees may not eat lunch or have their usual cup of coffee during the day.

Not all Muslims have to fast, however, particularly if they are ill or travelling. If a woman is menstruating, pregnant or breastfeeding, she is exempted from fasting. Similarly, if a person is travelling away from home to a distant place, he or she is not required to fast. They may fast later in the year instead. The elderly and the sick are also exempt. Instead, they may make up the missed days at a later time, or give charity to feed the needy. Children are expected to fast when they reach religious maturity: the beginning of menstruation for girls, and the onset of puberty for boys. Before this, children in many Muslim families may fast a day here and there until they become accustomed to the practice and can fast properly on reaching maturity.

As well as obligatory fasting during the month of Ramadan, Muslims are encouraged to perform voluntary fasts as a form of spiritual training. Some days are recommended for fasting, such as the six days in the week following Eid al-Fitr or the ninth, tenth and eleventh days of Muharram, the first month of the Islamic calendar. Some Muslims also fast on Mondays and Thursdays. Like voluntary prayers, these types of fasts are believed to help the person draw closer to God and to develop spiritually.

Giving charity (zakat)

The rituals of praying and fasting, discussed above, are intended to develop individual spirituality—that is, the benefits of these activities affect an individual directly. The following practice also benefits the individual spiritually, but it has a broader influence on other members of society.

Zakat is the payment of charity once a year by every Muslim who has a minimum level of savings. Several conditions should be met before one should pay the zakat. First, the person who has to pay zakat must be a Muslim and have reached puberty. Second, he or she must have a minimum amount of savings held for a minimum of one year, equivalent to approximately three ounces of gold. Since the price of gold varies from time to time, one has to calculate the value of three ounces of gold in currency (say, in Australian dollars) to arrive at the amount of savings each year. In arriving at this figure, one must include in it cash savings, as well as other assets such as shares and assets in a business, if any. Third, the person must have paid all their expenses for the year, including any debts.

The amount to be paid is 2.5 per cent of the average annual savings or wealth of the individual. This amount is usually paid to a government agency handling zakat (in some Muslim-majority countries) or to an organisation that distributes zakat funds. Some individuals prefer to distribute these funds themselves. The beneficiaries of zakat are many, including the poor, the needy, the disadvantaged who are struggling to repay their debts, new converts to Islam, orphans, widows and poor relatives, students, and general welfare projects such as educational institutions, mosques and hospitals.

As well, Muslims are asked to give a small amount at the end of Ramadan, in order to allow the poor to celebrate the end of fasting as well. In Australia, this could be under $10, and basically amounts to the price of a meal. This is paid on behalf of every member of the family before the Eid al-Fitr prayers, so that the whole community—rich and poor—may celebrate and share food together afterwards. Charity in Islam is not restricted to other Muslims only.

Apart from obligatory zakat, another common type of charity is the voluntary *sadaqa*, which simply refers to sharing what one has with those who have less. In many Muslim countries, sadaqa allows for the establishment of hospitals, schools and mosques, as well as free medical and educational services for the poor. The basic idea behind giving charity is that a person should be grateful and generous with whatever God has given them: be that money, knowledge, wisdom, physical ability or anything else. This cooperative ethic is important in Islam and is supposed to be an essential characteristic of an Islamic society. Stinginess is highly discouraged; generosity is encouraged.

Australian Muslims tend to pay their zakat individually, as there are no government institutions to handle the zakat funds. They give their zakat to mosques, Islamic societies, charities, and the poor and needy in the community.

Pilgrimage to Mecca (hajj)

At least once in a lifetime, as long as they are physically and financially able, every Muslim is expected to perform the pilgrimage to Mecca, called the hajj. Devout Muslims the world over eagerly await the day when they can fulfil this important ritual, many saving a lifetime for the journey. Those who can afford it may even perform the hajj more than once.

Muslims believe that the various rites connected with the hajj are associated with the Prophet Abraham, his wife Hagar and their son Ishmael. As mentioned previously, it is believed that Abraham and Ishmael constructed the sanctuary of the Ka'ba in Mecca. Although the various rites and rituals of the hajj have a symbolic connection to Abraham, Hagar and Ishmael, they are just that: symbols. In performing the rites, a Muslim's attention is directed to God, as worship of any person or thing other than God is forbidden in Islam.

Every year, during the twelfth and final month of the Islamic calendar, the pilgrimage season begins. More than two million Muslims normally attend. Male pilgrims don two pieces of white, seamless cloth, and women wear their normal clothes, making sure that their faces are uncovered. The purpose of everyone wearing simple clothes is to signify that all people are equal before God, no matter if they are rich or poor, black or white. In this sense, the hajj is the great equaliser, and pilgrims experience being among a mass of humanity from all the corners of the earth.

It takes about five days for the various hajj rituals to be completed, including visiting the Ka'ba and praying at the Grand

Mosque in Mecca; performing a procession between the hills of Safa and Marwa (now located inside the Grand Mosque) to commemorate Hagar's search for water; and the stoning of three pillars in Mina to symbolise the rejection of Satan. But the highlight of the hajj is on the ninth day of the month when all the pilgrims gather at a place called Arafat, near Mecca. It is considered the most blessed day of the pilgrimage and people spend their time praying, reflecting, supplicating and reciting the Qur'an. Everyone stands in repentance before God, and it is believed that if their hajj is accepted, their previous misdeeds and sins are washed away and forgiven.

From Arafat they move to another area close to Mecca called Muzdalifa, where they spend the night. In the morning of the tenth day of the month, they move to an area called Mina. This day is the day of Eid al-Ad ha, the day of feasting.

On this day, pilgrims sacrifice a sheep, cow or camel in order to feed the poor. There are specially built slaughter-houses close to Mecca for this purpose. Hundreds of thousands of animals are slaughtered during the pilgrimage, and today their meat is packaged and distributed to the poor and needy in all corners of the world. The pilgrim does not have to be physically present at the slaughter-house; the management of the slaughter-house handles the actual slaughtering. Male pilgrims then shave or trim their hair and wear normal clothes again. They remain in Mina for another two or three days, before once again visiting the Ka'ba for a farewell circumambulation. Although it is not required, Muslims also visit Medina, where the Prophet Muhammad is buried.

When the pilgrim returns to their home, they receive the

title 'Haji' for men or 'Hajja' for women, which indicates that they have completed the pilgrimage, and are received with much fanfare and festivity. Someone who has completed the hajj is given a special status in the community.

Those performing hajj may only use *halal* (lawful) means to do so. If they have gone to the hajj using funds acquired illegally (such as through bribery, stealing, misappropriation or cheating) then their hajj will not be accepted by God and will be considered worthless. Many Muslims have reported undergoing a spiritual transformation as a result of performing the hajj: they feel that they have become more connected with God. Muslims have spoken about the feelings of joy, elation, awe and humility at having the opportunity to fulfil this fundamental Islamic duty. They also experience a sense of oneness with humanity, as pilgrims from all around the globe gather in peace and unity to worship God.

After having completed a hajj, Muslims may also perform the voluntary pilgrimage known as *umra*. Like the performance of other voluntary rituals of prayer, fasting and giving charity, umra helps Muslims in the process of constantly refining and reforming themselves as part of their spiritual journey to God.

Many Australian Muslims also perform hajj each year. Special hajj trips are organised by community groups or travel agencies to facilitate the performance of hajj as comfortably as possible.

Chapter 5

UNITY AND DIVERSITY

Perhaps more than any other single factor, Muslims in Australia are marked by their ethnic diversity. Muslim migration to Australia was, and is, from a variety of nation states themselves possessing distinct cultural and ethnic groups. Migrants coming to Australia bring not only their religious faith, but also their cultural identities with them, and quite often these cultural identities figure as strongly as the religious identity. Muslims also vary in their degree of commitment to Islam as well as in their approaches to it.

There are further differences in the level of integration into Australian society, particularly among the second and third generation Muslims. Complicating all this is also the existence of an increasing number of converts to Islam from European backgrounds who were born and grew up in Australia. Thus not all Muslims share the same views on all issues, and often there is no one standard 'Islamic' view on many of the problems and issues Muslims face in their daily lives.

UNDERSTANDING THE THREE TIERS OR LEVELS OF 'ISLAM'

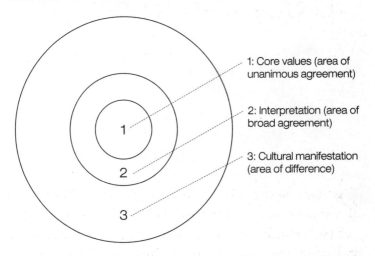

1: Core values (area of unanimous agreement)

2: Interpretation (area of broad agreement)

3: Cultural manifestation (area of difference)

In order to understand what makes a Muslim Muslim and what does not, it is important to look at what is known as 'Islam'. This term is often misused and misunderstood, quite often being confused with the cultural practices of a particular ethnic group. Some do not make a distinction between core values and beliefs in Islam and the cultural manifestation of these core values and beliefs in different Muslim communities.

It is possible to understand 'Islam' in terms of three tiers or levels:

- Level I: Core values, beliefs, ideas and institutions.

- Level 2: Interpretation of these core values, beliefs, ideas and institutions to enable putting them into practice.
- Level 3: Cultural manifestation of these core values, beliefs, ideas and institutions, in different contexts.

At the first level, that is, Islam's core values, beliefs, ideas and institutions, there is broad agreement among all Muslims. This first inner level is quite small and contains only the most basic beliefs and practices upon which there is no disagreement such as the idea of the oneness of God; that the Prophet Muhammad is the last Messenger in a line of continuous prophecy from Adam; that the Qur'an is the word of God; that Muslims must pray the five daily prayers, fast during Ramadan, give zakat and perform the hajj if they are physically and financially able; that pork and alcohol are prohibited and that murder and adultery are forbidden. The second level is the interpretation of these core values to enable putting them into practice. Broader than the first level, Muslims may have minor differences of opinion at this second level. But there is broad agreement on this inter-pretation. The third level is the cultural manifestation of Islam and it is here that there are substantial differences among the Muslims.

To provide an example of the three levels at work, we can look at the prayer (salat).

- Level 1: There is unanimous agreement that Muslims must pray the five daily prayers and on the basic features of prayer.
- Level 2: There are minor differences of opinion on exactly how some of the actions of the prayer are to be performed.

- Level 3: The type, colour and make of clothes a believer wears while praying differ widely according to taste and custom.

Australian Muslims, generally speaking, agree on Level 1 but may differ widely on Level 3.

DIVERSITY AMONG AUSTRALIAN MUSLIMS

Sunnis and Shi'is

One of the most significant divisions occurred very early on in Muslim history when there was debate over who should succeed the Prophet as leader of the Muslim community. Some Muslims (later to be known as Shi'is) felt that the family of the Prophet should be given preference. Other Muslims (later to be known as Sunnis), who appeared to be in the majority, argued that political succession had nothing to do with the family of the Prophet as such, and that the office was open to anyone capable of handling it. The differences between the two groups widened over the centuries and took on theological connotations, but initially the distinction was merely connected to political succession.

While the majority of the Muslim population in Australia is Sunni, a large number of migrants from Iraq, Lebanon and Iran are Shi'is. Within each group, there are legal, theological and ideological differences. Despite such sharp differences, prominent in the countries of origin, there appears to be a tendency on the part of both Shi'is and Sunnis in Australia to narrow their differences and come to a more common view of their identity as Muslims. Although there is somewhat of a sense of togetherness in a number of areas, the two groups still maintain some distinctions. Shi'i Muslims have their own mosques and schools, for example, and Sunni Muslims their own as well. However, at times Sunnis and Shi'is may share the same mosque for prayers and other social and religious functions.

Theological divisions

Australian Muslims differ along theological lines. Although many Muslims do not get into debates on 'theological' issues, the same trends seen among Muslims elsewhere in the Muslim world exist in Australia. Australian Muslims would give answers to these and similar questions based on their theological orientation:

- How are we to understand what God is, and His attributes such as 'Merciful', 'All-knowing', 'Compassionate'?
- What is the role of reason in Islam?
- Did God 'create' both good and evil?
- Do human beings have free will?
- Are human beings 'forced' to be bad or good?

Legal divisions: Schools of law

Apart from theological diversity, there are differences among Australian Muslims on questions of Islamic law. For example, on the question of the role of women, Australian Muslims differ among themselves as to what it should be. Are male and female roles equivalent? Do women have a special role? What is their place in society? There are also differences on how to perform the five daily prayers. While there is agreement over the major aspects, Muslims still differ with each other on minor points. If this is the case with something as basic as prayer, then it is only natural that Muslims would differ on issues such as human rights, war and peace, and other issues of interest to us today, just like any other religious group.

All of the major Islamic legal schools are represented in Australia. The three schools mostly followed are the Hanafi, the Shafi'i and Ja'fari. The Hanafi legal school is followed by Muslims from India, Pakistan, Afghanistan, Lebanon and Turkey, and the Shafi'i school by those from Indonesia, Malaysia and Egypt. The Ja'fari school is followed by Shi'i Muslims from Iran, Iraq, Afghanistan and Lebanon.

Spirituality and Sufis

There are differences among Muslims on the degree of emphasis one should place on the spiritual dimension of Islam, often referred to as 'Sufism' (that is, Islamic mysticism). A significant number of Australian Muslims are associated in one way or another with Sufi orders (or organisations) that provide methods for refining the soul and helping the seeker in his or her quest to 'reach' God. The Sufi path, in general, involves meditation, prayer, chanting, selfless love of others and renunciation of certain aspects of the material world. The Sufi develops through a variety of exercises: thankfulness to God, patience, reliance on God, fear of God and love of God. Each Sufi order has its specific guidelines, instructions and practices, which help the person achieve the objective of refining the soul and 'reaching'

God. In Australia, a number of Sufi orders are followed. In Melbourne, Sydney and Brisbane, for instance, Sufi circles are often found with their weekly gatherings in mosques and prayer facilities. In Canberra, there is a centre for promoting Sufism. The so-called 'Whirling Dervishes' of the Mevlewiyya order also have some presence. In fact, European converts to Islam are often attracted to various Sufi orders.

Converts and non-converts

Australia's Muslim community is seeing the creation of a significant number of converts to Islam from European and other backgrounds. Although this phenomenon is not entirely new, as interest in Islam goes back to the 1960s, there were few converts at that time. However, since the 1980s there have been an increasing number of Australians converting to Islam.

There are several reasons for conversion. In some cases it is precipitated by marriage, particularly when the prospective wife is a Muslim. Classical Islamic law does not permit marriage between a Muslim woman and a non-Muslim man, and in cases where the couple elects to respect the wishes of the woman or her parents, the non-Muslim man may convert, by conviction or otherwise. In some instances it may be a superficial conversion, and there are reports in Australia of husbands who return to their original faith after marriage. But in other cases the conversion is permanent and the convert remains a practising Muslim. While classical Islamic law allows the marriage of a Muslim man to a Christian or Jewish woman without her being required to abandon her faith, there are also instances of non-Muslim women converting to Islam after meeting and marrying Muslim men.

Marriage is not the sole reason why Australians are embracing Islam. In the course of contact and friendship with Muslims, and through learning about the religion, its teachings and history, some Australians convert to Islam. There are also suggestions that Islamic spirituality is an important factor in conversion.

These Australian Muslims have become active in communities both in formal organisational roles and through informal networks of friends. The Melbourne-based 'Reverts Support Group' runs a variety of social and educational gatherings and has produced, for example, a prayer kit for new Muslims.

Those who are committed to Islam and those who are not

The Muslim community in Australia, like any other Muslim community in the world, has followers with varying degrees of commitment to Islam. There are those who are fully committed to Islam and are interested in manifesting Islamic ideas, values and practices in their lives. While it is difficult to gain an idea of exactly how many Muslims would fall into this category, judging by what is happening elsewhere in the world we might say that between 30 to 40 per cent of Muslims could be defined in this way. This is an educated guess, nothing more. Some Muslims are not particularly interested in being religious and see Islam merely as an aspect of their cultural identification rather than a living faith that they practise. Another 30 to 40 per cent of Muslims probably fall into this category. A small number of Muslims may even demonstrate a degree of hostility towards Islam.

Approaches to modern issues and challenges

Like their co-religionists elsewhere, Australian Muslims differ among themselves on questions dealing with many of the issues and challenges that Muslims are facing in the modern period. Examples of questions commonly raised are:

- What is an Islamic state? Is it necessary for Muslims to establish one?
- Are Islam and 'the West' mutually exclusive or is there an overlapping relationship?
- To what extent should Muslims adopt or reject so-called Western ideas and values, or is it possible to find a compromise?
- Are human rights as specified in the Universal Declaration of Human Rights (1948) compatible with Islam?
- Are calls for emancipation of women in line with Islamic ideas of justice and fairness?
- Is the interest-based financial system compatible with Islamic teachings on the prohibition of exploitation and usury?

For instance, on the question of establishing an Islamic state, Australian Muslims disagree on whether it is an important issue.

- Some Muslims believe it is essential for Muslims where they form a majority to establish an Islamic state where Islamic law is implemented.

- Some Muslims totally reject the idea of an Islamic state as nothing more than an authoritarian or autocratic religious theocracy.

- For most Muslims in Australia, the debate on Islamic state is irrelevant. First, Muslims are a small minority and even if they wanted they cannot have what is called an Islamic state here. Secondly, the Australian state allows total freedom for Muslims to practice their religion and therefore there is no need for an alternative 'state' or a system. From their point of view, Muslims in Australia can function perfectly well as Muslims and Australians without an Islamic state.

Trends within Australian Islam

Australian Muslims (men and women) can also be divided into four main trends of thought with respect to their approach to modern issues and challenges as well as to classical Islamic law. The following divisions merely highlight the broad approach of each trend of thought. In practice, many sub-groups exist within each.

- **Traditionalists:** Some Muslims argue that the classical formulations in Islamic law are just as relevant as they have ever been and that the answers provided in these classical formulations should be sufficient to meet modern challenges. These Muslims rely on the weight and authority of tradition to justify their positions. Examples of Traditionalists in Australia include the Salafis, who are heavily influenced by the teachings of scholars like Ibn Taymiyya and Muhammad

b. Abd al-Wahhab, as well as those Muslims who strictly follow the classical schools of law.

- **Neo-Modernists:** Some Muslims argue for reform in classical Islamic law and adoption of many of the ideas and institutions emanating from the West. They do not believe that there is any inherent conflict between Islam and modernity.

- **Neo-Revivalists:** Yet other Muslims feel that Western civilisation is essentially anti-religious and, in particular, anti-Islamic. They argue it is based on a materialistic conception of the world, which excludes God and religion from public life, ideas unacceptable to Islam. They argue for some degree of reform of classical Islamic law and thought. They also call for Islamisation of institutions and systems in society, where possible, such as those of the economic and financial. Examples of neo-Revivalists include Muslims who have been heavily influenced by the work of the Pakistani thinker Abu'l Ala Mawdudi and the Egyptian reformer Hasan al-Banna.

- **Liberals:** Yet another trend among Muslims argues for a more liberal approach to Islam. They feel that many of the traditional ideas, values and institutions developed during the classical period were highly dependent on the socio-political and historical circumstances of the time, and therefore may not necessarily be relevant for the modern period. While they argue for the retention of the core ideas, beliefs and institutions of Islam—such as the oneness of God and the prophethood of Muhammad, the five daily prayers and so on—they argue that 'inspiration' from the Qur'an, the traditions of the Prophet and early Islamic history, could be the basis on which to develop new ideas, institutions and values compatible with the needs of Muslims in the modern world. These Muslims are not literalistic in their reading of the Islamic source texts. Examples in Australia include those referred to as 'secular' or 'modernist' Muslims.

An issue that illustrates the various approaches that Australian Muslims take is the role of Muslim women in Australian society:

- **Traditionalists** rely on classical ideas about 'status of women' or 'role of women' and narrow down the options available for women rather than allowing them a major role in society. Therefore, ideas of segregation dominate traditionalist discourse.
- **Neo-Modernists** argue that in the modern period, there is no need to adopt some of the classical formulations, and as men and women are equal there is no reason why women should not play as substantial a role in society as men.
- **Neo-Revivalists** try to draw from the Qur'an and the traditions of the Prophet what they consider to be the 'pure Islamic' ideas about women's roles. They argue that women should not be completely excluded from public life. But in practice, the role they assign to women is considerably narrowed. Their position comes very close to that of Traditionalists.
- **Liberals** argue that as society has changed considerably, the practices of the first generation of Muslims do not need to be emulated in order to satisfy modern circumstances and needs. For them, the spirit underlying the message of the Qur'an and the traditions of the Prophet is an essentially liberating one, and should be the force guiding Muslims in

their attempt to reformulate the role of women in society. On that basis, they argue that in today's environment, women and men play a more or less equal role. For this reason, there is no need to restrict women's activities in public areas, such as in politics, education, the military, or general society. Their position is more in line with current debate on the role of women in the West, and part of a global discourse, albeit one functioning within a broader Islamic framework. Their approach moves away from literalist readings of Islam towards seeking inspiration from Islamic source texts.

Beyond the issue of women's rights, any important issue Muslims are facing today can be covered by this spectrum of approaches. Examples of such debates and issues among Muslims in Australia (as evidenced by magazines, websites and discussion groups) include interfaith and cross-cultural marriages; political alliance with non-Muslims; religious extremism and fanaticism; separation of church and state; secularism; dress codes and Muslim identity; globalisation; traditional family patterns; interest-based banking and finance; and music.

We can see that on every single issue of importance to Muslims today, there are many views and opinions, and that while some groups believe it is their view that is representative of Islam, others might heartily disagree.

Whose view is the 'Islamic' one?

There is no central authoritative body or institution among Muslims to determine precisely what is Islamic and what is not. Muslims do not have a figure such as the Pope, to determine which interpretation of the Qur'an or the traditions of the Prophet is correct. In a sense, then, Islam is a rather democratic religion when it comes to determining what is acceptable and what is not, because potentially everyone has a say in it, so to speak. In practice, it is the scholars of religion who have studied the Qur'an, the traditions, the history, the civilisation and customs of Muslims, who have the most important say. But even then, they speak and act only as individuals, and cannot enforce their opinions on the whole Muslim community, neither around the world nor even in a particular locality.

Chapter 6

THE LIFE CYCLE
OF A MUSLIM

In this chapter we will look at the life cycle of a Muslim from birth, through to marriage, the raising of children and caring for the elderly, and finally what happens when a Muslim dies. Much of what follows varies from culture to culture and, within Australia, from one ethnic community to another. Thus, a generalised picture of what happens in all Australian Muslim communities is difficult to paint. However, most Muslims will be familiar with the broad outlines presented here, although they may disagree on specifics.

BIRTH

Muslims celebrate the birth of a child in many different ways according to the culture into which he or she is born. However, one practice common to Muslims is the call to prayer (adhan) immediately, or as soon as possible, after the birth of the baby.

This is performed by a member of the family, the local imam or another religious figure, and involves softly making the 'call to prayer' in the right ear of the baby and the 'call to commence prayer' in the left ear. In this way, the first words a new baby hears are those calling the faithful to worship. It is hoped that the baby will then carry the sense of the sacred with him or her throughout life. Given that in Australia, Muslim women, like others, have their babies delivered in hospital, it can be some-what difficult for the Muslim family to put into practice this ritual as undertaken elsewhere in the Muslim world.

NAMING CEREMONY

Usually on the seventh day of a child's life, Australian Muslims have a naming ceremony called *'aqiqa*. While specific practices do vary, usually a name is given to the child and their hair is shaved. Gifts and charity are given to the disadvantaged in the com-munity, and for this purpose a sheep or goat is ordered from the butcher. Part of the meat is cooked and shared with friends and relatives, with the other part being given away to the poor and needy. The 'aqiqa is a time of celebration and giving thanks to God for the gift of a new child.

Yusuf, Annee and Ilyas: Having an 'Aqiqa

The 'aqiqa is a Muslim tradition that celebrates the birth of a new baby. After the birth of our son Ilyas, we wanted the 'aqiqa to be a warm welcome for him into the world. There were around

70 people, who were a fairly even mix of Muslims and non-Muslims. It was a warm afternoon and we all sat outside in the garden, where we had prepared a large feast. We all had a wonderful time eating and talking to each other. On that day, many got their first chance to see baby Ilyas, who observed the afternoon quietly from his mother's arms. Ilyas's 'aqiqa was a very enjoyable day for everyone.

CIRCUMCISION

Australian Muslims, like Muslims elsewhere, practise circumcision for boys. This involves removing the foreskin of the penis and is carried out by a doctor at the hospital. There is no requirement for the doctor to be Muslim. Usually in Australia a boy is circumcised very early in his life, but in some cultures elsewhere in the Muslim world, circumcision takes place much later, even after six years. Like the 'aqiqa, it is a happy occasion and often celebrated with presents, visits from family and sharing of food.

A very common misunderstanding is that Muslim girls are required to undergo a process known as female circumcision, also called female genital mutilation or female genital cutting. There is no instruction from either the Prophet or the Qur'an which requires such a thing and it is not common among Muslims. The practice does exist in some cultures, but it is a local phenomenon common to all the religions of the region in which it exists. In most Muslim cultures around the world, female circumcision is not practised, and where it is practised it can vary from a symbolic act that does not require any cutting or mutilation to genital mutilation. In Australia, female circumcision is not a common practice among Muslims.

LEARNING ABOUT RELIGION

Right from early childhood, a Muslim child begins to learn about the religion. Initially, the child learns how to recite some short chapters (*sura*) of the Qur'an, and the occasion of memorising parts of the Qur'an is celebrated. As well, the child learns how to pray through watching their parents and other siblings, and taking part at times. In mosques, it is quite common to see young toddlers copying their parents in the movements of prayer, or wandering in and out of the rows of worshippers. A Muslim child also grows up learning which activities are permissible and which are prohibited in Islam. In this way, the child learns how to be a Muslim from early childhood.

Australian Muslims often send their children to a mosque or a weekend school to learn how to read the Qur'an and about the religion. But many other Muslim children in Australia grow up without knowing much about their religion. The parents' lack of interest in religion, their inability to devote time to teaching the child the basics, not having the time to take the child to a weekend school, or simply the fact that they reside in areas where there is no Muslim community facility, are problems commonly cited. Many parents who are new arrivals in Australia may find it difficult to settle down, get a job and work extended hours in order to survive and thus may find little time to attend to the religious education needs of their children unless they themselves are committed practising Muslims.

Many Muslim youngsters thus become aware of Islam and its teachings only after leaving school. For example, Muslim students at university may be introduced to Islam through the activities of Muslim student organisations which organise Qur'an classes, study circles and lectures for this purpose.

REACHING PUBERTY

When children reach puberty, they are considered to have entered the world of adults and are expected to perform the various rituals of Islam, such as the five daily prayers, and fasting during Ramadan. By then, the child will have had plenty of time to become familiar with the rituals and may even have begun to try them already. Muslim children are usually praying by the ages of seven or eight, and may perform a few days of fasting by then as well. At puberty, a child is considered to have the ability to differentiate between right and wrong and must therefore undertake to perform their religious obligations for the rest of their life. Unlike some religious traditions, there are no particular celebratory rituals which Muslim children are expected to perform on reaching puberty.

MARRIAGE

Theoretically, puberty is also the time when marriage becomes permissible. In practice, marriage is usually deferred in almost all Muslim societies until at least the age of sixteen or seventeen, or even later in Australia. The general attitude, however, even in Australia, is to encourage early marriage (see table opposite). One reason is that Islam strictly prohibits sex outside the confines of marriage, and marrying early helps to prevent young adults from falling into illicit sexual relationships. In line with this, Australian Muslims (both male and female) tend to marry much earlier than the overall Australian population.

Percentage of Muslims who are married compared to the overall Australian population, 1996

Age group	Males— Muslim	Males— OAP*	Females— Muslim	Females— OAP*
	Australian population		Australian population	
15–19 years	1.0	0.4	8.1	1.0
20–24 years	18.2	7.3	50.3	15.8
25–29 years	52.8	34.0	73.9	47.2
30–34 years	71.8	56.7	80.9	64.5

Source: Australian Bureau of Statistics, 1996 Census

*OAP: Overall Australia Population

If we compare the Muslim males and females, a higher percentage of Muslim females marry much earlier than Muslim males. For instance, for the age group 15–19 years, only 1 per cent of the Muslim males are married compared to 8.1 per cent of females. This trend continues in the other age groups. It is a pattern one finds in a number of Muslim communities outside Australia as well.

Because the young adults are less experienced, in many Muslim cultures, even in Australia, parents often play a significant role in helping them to make marriage-related decisions. They will also be supported and helped by older members of the extended families.

There is a perception in Australia that arranged marriages

are common among Australian Muslims and that often young adults are forced into these marriages. It is true that arranged marriages are very common in some Muslim cultures (in the Indian subcontinent, for example), where parents will explore potential matches, assess the suitability of the pair, and come to some sort of understanding with the potential in-laws. The young adults are then consulted and, if all agree, the marriage is contracted. However, it is also true that arranged marriages can be misused, and young couples may be forced into a marriage in which they are not interested, despite the fact that the teachings of the Prophet are against the idea of forcing young adults into marriages they do not want to enter into.

In Australia, arranged marriage does not appear to be a common practice among Muslims. However, among migrants coming from cultures where arranged marriage is common, there may be a tendency on the part of some to retain this institution in some form (in a much diluted fashion to accommodate the laws in Australia, as well as to give a stronger say to the young adults).

One form of 'arranged marriage' that exists among Australian Muslims is where a Muslim (male or female) approaches other members of the Muslim community or an imam seeking a marriage partner. Imams, community leaders and friends do play a significant role in this from time to time.

In Islam, marriage is a commitment of a man and a woman to each other; it is a contract in which both are considered complementary partners. Among Australian Muslims, particularly second and third generation Muslims, there is a strong belief that there should not be any domination by one party of the

Rafiq and Maryam:
A Muslim marriage ceremony

When it came to our wedding, the adage that 'you can't please all of the people all of the time' did not apply. We wanted to honour ourselves, our family, our past and our present, to abide by the laws of Australia, and, most importantly, to honour our Creator and Sustainer. We knew this might be an impossible dream as so many people have their own idea of what constitutes a wedding and can get upset when the event takes another course. Would past friends accept no alcohol at the reception? Would our parents consider the head covering of the bride oppressive? Would Muslim friends reject readings from the Bible as un-Islamic?

Our answer was to be true to ourselves and let the wedding be a celebration of how God has brought us together. We started the ceremony with the evocative words 'You who love lovers, this is your home. Welcome!!' by the Persian poet and mystic Rumi. Although people came from different backgrounds, traditions and cultures, they did 'love lovers' and in that spirit we achieved our dreams.

other in marriage. In order to safeguard the interests of both parties, the marriage contract can contain clauses inserted by either partner to stipulate conditions that must be respected in the marriage and to clarify any areas of doubt between the two individuals. The idea, however, is for a man and a woman to grow close together in a common bond, complementing and supporting each other and leading to children as a result. However, despite the teachings of the Qur'an and the Prophet, in some Muslim cultures, the idea of the wife being subservient to the husband still exists. It is difficult to generalise about this issue, and local cultural factors play a major role in determining the nature of the relationship between a man and a woman in marriage and the relative power of each. In Western countries such as Australia, the tendency among many Muslims is to adopt the views that are prevalent in the community about the equality of man and woman and to emphasise that the relationship is more of a cooperative one than one of domination.

Since this firm commitment to one another is vital, Islam does not condone what are seen as 'temporary' arrangements, such as de facto relationships. Marriage, in Islam, means full and total commitment to each other and is not conditional upon a time limit or contracted on a trial basis.

The family

In Islam, marriage is expected to lead to the creation of a family. The traditional pattern of a husband, wife and children is considered the basic unit of society.

Blood ties are considered perhaps the strongest of bonds. A child's link to his or her parents, grandparents, uncles, aunts, nieces, nephews, and so on, is considered a very important aspect of family life. The family in most Muslim cultures includes these extended relatives. In traditional Muslim societies, all are linked to each other, with the bonds being maintained throughout life.

In Islam, parents are accorded high respect, something the Qur'an stresses in a number of places, for instance:

And do good unto [thy] parents. Should one of them, or both, attain to old age in thy care, never say 'Ugh' to them or scold them, but [always] speak unto them with reverent speech, and spread over them humbly the wings of thy tenderness, and say: 'O my Sustainer! Bestow Thy grace upon them, even as they cherished and reared me when I was a child!' (Qur'an 17:23–24)

This love and care is particularly given to the mother, partly due to the close bond that develops between a mother and her children, but also because the norms of Islamic behaviour accord the mother an extremely high place. The Prophet was reported to have said: 'Paradise is at the feet of mothers.'

It is expected that both the mother and father will contribute to the care and upbringing of their young. Child rearing is the duty of both parents, and fathers are expected to contribute, not only materially, but in other ways as well. Parents have a duty to provide a safe environment so that their children can grow up in a psychologically balanced state. It is also their responsibility to teach them Islamic values and norms of behaviour, as well as the proper conduct of individuals within the family and broader society. They are expected to teach their children the religion so that at maturity they become Muslims who accept and put into practice the teachings of Islam. The education of children is therefore a weighty obligation for parents. Parents should also ensure that their children receive training and skills in order for them to contribute to their own development and that of the wider community, and there is a Muslim tradition stating that seeking knowledge is a sacred duty for every male and female.

Following the Prophet's example and guidance, children should be loved and cherished. There are many stories showing how deeply the Prophet loved his children and grandchildren. Once, a companion noticed the Prophet lovingly kissing his grandson, Hassan, and stated that he had never kissed any of his ten children. The Prophet gave him a look and replied: 'Whoever is not merciful to others will not be treated mercifully.'

So, children should be given moral, social and spiritual attention in order for them to grow up as balanced human beings with their own identities, but who also are aware of their responsibilities towards the family and the wider community. The values, morals and norms of Muslim behaviour are called *akhlaq* and are an important aspect of the education of children in Muslim societies.

Family planning

In a number of Muslim societies, the tendency is to have large families, while in others family planning is widely practised with the support of religious authorities. Family planning programs of the 1960s and 1970s, for instance, were highly successful in Indonesia while they failed miserably in Pakistan, both Muslim-majority countries. Religious authorities in Indonesia were behind the government's family planning program, giving it religious sanction. In Pakistan, however, there was no such cooperation. The religious establishments in Pakistan considered family planning against Islamic teachings, while in Indonesia it was not considered to be so. Conflicting views exist among Muslims, therefore, on issues such as family planning.

In Australia, while some Muslims tend to have large families, others go for a smaller family. There does not seem to be particular pattern among Muslims in general. Ethnicity, class, generation and education all seem to play a part in this. Family planning is an issue that is not widely discussed or debated among Muslims in Australia. It seems that most Muslims are comfortable with using various means of contraception.

Abortion

Classical Muslim scholars were rather liberal in their judgments on the topic of abortion, but these days the general tendency among Australian Muslims is to consider abortion prohibited unless there is an immediate danger to the life of the mother. If a recognised medical authority detects that such a danger exists, an abortion may be performed within a certain period of time. While this is the ideal, the practice may vary from person to person. Like many other similar issues, commitment to religious values and degree of familiarity with the relevant teachings play a significant role in making such decisions, as it is relatively easy in Australia to get an abortion.

Debates on abortion in the wider community also influence this debate among Muslims in Australia, and it is often the Right to Life argument against abortion which is taken up.

DIVORCE

If circumstances lead to irreconcilable differences and the partners in a marriage simply cannot live with each other, divorce is considered permissible as a last resort after all other means for resolving the problem have been exhausted. Indicating the seriousness of a marriage break-up, there is an Islamic tradition that refers to divorce as the most hated of permissible things in the sight of God. Despite this ideal, the practice among Australian Muslims is that the divorce rate among both males and females (aged 15 to 29 years) is higher than for the overall Australian population. Perhaps this has a lot to do with the fact that a higher percentage of young Muslims marry earlier than the overall Australian population.

From 30 years and above, interestingly, the divorce rate among both male and female Muslims is lower than that among the overall Australian population.

MUSLIM YOUTH

The idea that at the age of eighteen, a young adult should leave his or her home and live independently, unless they are married, does not seem to be acceptable to most Muslims in Australia. In fact, young Muslims over eighteen usually live with their parents until they get married and start a new life of their own. Parents are expected to support their children until they are able to stand on their own. Thus, it is common for parents to pay for their children's university education and to support them until they graduate and find employment. Parents, children and siblings, and close relatives are expected to support each other at any age in time of need. Thus, the family is still the most important safety net for many young adults, despite the availability of support systems provided by the government.

In order to cater for the needs of Muslim youth, in the 1980s and 1990s a large number of Muslim youth groups emerged in almost all capital cities in Australia. While many other areas of Muslim community activities are organised around an ethnic group or a particular locality, these youth groups are more likely to be multi-ethnic. Examples include the Young Muslims of Australia and the Federation of Australian Muslim Youth (in New South Wales), the Young Muslims of Australia and the Federation of Australian Muslim Students and Youth (in Victoria), and Muslim students' associations and societies based in university campuses throughout Australia.

Muslim youth in Australia, like all other young people, have their fair share of problems: homelessness, drugs, delinquency and crime. However, there is no research to back up the view that these problems are more prominent in Muslim communities than in the overall Australian population. When Muslims are concentrated in certain areas such as Lakemba in Sydney or Campbellfield in Melbourne, some crimes committed by members of a particular ethnic group—say, Lebanese Australians in Lakemba or Turkish Australians in Campbellfield—tend to get media attention. References to Lebanese or Turkish 'gangs' and 'gang activity' are then made. Crime becomes connected to one's ethnicity, and since Lebanese and Turks are often associated with Islam, religion is also dragged into the debate. It then becomes 'ethnic crime' or 'Muslim crime'.

Of all the problems Muslim youth faces, the drug problem seems to be among the most challenging, as it is for Australian young people generally. While the solution to the drug problem cannot be reduced to a few religious exhortations, Muslim youth groups do play their role in utilising religion and its teachings to bring the offenders back to a drug-free life, wherever possible.

The success of some American Muslim community leaders in tackling the drug problem in their neighbourhoods in places like New York is viewed by Australian Muslim leaders as a good example. Zachariah Matthews, an active member of the Muslim community on youth issues, in a talk given on 'Muslim Youth and Drugs' at the Cabramatta Mosque, reinforces the message given to Muslim youth in many youth circles:

> Dare to be different—a Muslim—and proud of it.
>
> Hang out with good company—fellow believers who will encourage you to do right.
>
> Avoid the trash music corrupting your innocent minds.
>
> Be careful about what programs you watch on TV.
>
> Avoid being in the presence of intoxicants (especially alcohol)—for example, pubs, social gatherings, dance parties, and so on—the temptation is always there.

He reminded his audience that the drug problem among Muslim youth has to be tackled as a community: by parents, religious and community leaders and young people themselves with the support of the state.

THE ELDERLY

From birth, to marriage, to growing old, a support network of family is expected to surround the Muslim throughout life. In many Muslim cultures, elderly parents live with their children, reflecting that it is considered in Islam an obligation on the part of children to take care of their parents when necessary. This duty is taken so seriously that to neglect it is seen as a major sin for which a person will be accountable on the Day of Judgment.

To facilitate this care when parents are old, extended families often attempt to live together or side by side, and when young men marry, they usually bring their wives to the home of their parents. In many Muslim societies today, living together as part of an extended family is not always possible. In Australia, often young couples prefer to stay on their own, while keeping in touch with their parents and other family members on a regular basis.

Elderly Muslims face roughly the same challenges as any other elderly people in Australia face. Lack of appropriate accommodation and other facilities is a common problem. In most capitals, clubs and facilities are available, but these are often used only by men. In Victoria the Islamic Society of Melbourne Eastern Region runs a retirement home in Lysterfield, while the Turkish community runs the Turkish Hostel, located in Broadmeadows. In Queensland, the Islamic Women's Association of Queensland runs a facility for the elderly.

DEATH

When a Muslim is close to dying, someone near to them gently recites the shahada to ensure that the last thing a person says is the declaration of faith ('There is no god but God and Muhammad is the Messenger of God'). When the person dies, the body is washed thoroughly, usually by the husband or wife, or another family member of the same sex. It is then wrapped in three to five pieces of plain cloth and buried within a day or so. Being buried sooner rather than later is important. Normally the body is expected to be buried within 24 hours of death. But in Australia, given the legal requirements, this may not be possible and Muslims follow the legal requirements. If a post-mortem is legally necessary, this must be explained to the relatives. It is not a common practice among Muslims except in exceptional circumstances, given the teaching that the body of the dead has to be treated with the utmost respect. But Muslims, like other Australians, respect and follow Australian laws and regulations in this.

The person is expected to be buried in the place (town or city) where he or she dies. Cremation is prohibited. In some Muslim societies, particularly in dry, hot areas, coffins are not used. If one is, it should be simple rather than expensive, and tombstones and gravestones are not recommended. Following the burial, before leaving the graveyard, those present, led by an imam, will supplicate to God asking Him to forgive the deceased and to have mercy on him or her.

It is not encouraged to incur great costs for the funeral and burial. Underlying the idea of a simple burial is the belief that the family—already in grief—should not be further burdened by having to arrange an elaborate ceremony. Members of the Muslim community, friends and relatives visit the family of the deceased to offer condolences for three days following the death. Some Muslims invite members of the community to their houses for the purpose of reciting certain parts of the Qur'an, remembering God and praying for the deceased, after which food will usually be served.

Chapter 7

SACRED TIMES AND PLACES

SACRED TIMES IN ISLAM

Throughout a Muslim's life, important times are celebrated with various rituals. Whether it is through the five periods for daily prayer, the movement of the moon marking the Islamic calandar, or the dawn signalling the commencement of fasting during Ramadan, the rhythm of a Muslim's life is regulated physically and spiritually. A Muslim should always be conscious that time is a precious gift from God. Muslims are urged not to waste time or be idle. Rather, they should be aware of the passage of time and utilise it in ways which are beneficial both to the individual and to society. This does not mean that a Muslim is required to be an ascetic, or always engaged in busy activity. Islam teaches that Muslims should maintain a balance in their lives between prayer, work, social relations and recreation.

There are many special times in a person's life. At puberty, a person is expected to perform all the religious duties of an adult, such as prayer and fasting. Another special time is when a person gets married and has children of his or her own. Reaching old age and becoming an elder in the community is also highly respected and considered a natural part of life. Finally, at death, a person's connection to this world is ended and they begin a new chapter in their existence.

The Islamic calendar is composed of twelve months of 29–30 days, following the cycle of the moon. The Islamic calendar did not begin with the birth of the Prophet, or even with the beginning of his mission when he first began receiving revelations from God. It begins with the event of the migration of the Prophet from Mecca to Medina, known as the hijra, in 622 (see Chapter 2). Because of the importance of this event, the second caliph Umar ibn al-Khattab took this as Year I of the Islamic calendar, after the death of the Prophet, and Muslims began to date their time from then. Thus, Year I in the Islamic calendar is equivalent to 622 in the western Gregorian calendar. Presently, we are in the fifteenth century of the Islamic calendar. In dates, 'AH' is used to indicate that the date is according to the Islamic calendar, 'H' referring to the hijra (migration). For instance, Year I of the Islamic calendar is written as '1 AH'. The months of the Islamic calendar (in Arabic) are as follows:

1 Muharram
2 Safar
3 Rabi' al-Awwal
4 Rabi' al-Thani
5 Jumada al-Ula
6 Jumada al-Thaniya

7   Rajab

8   Sha'ban

9   Ramadan

10 Shawwal

11 Dhu al-Qa'ida

12 Dhu al-Hijja

Muslims in Australia often use the Islamic and Gregorian calendars *simultaneously*. Special calendars that use both calendars and list all the important Islamic days are available from mosques, Islamic centres, halal meat shops and Islamic bookshops.

Mosques also supply prayer timetables which list the times for each prayer for each month. Since the prayer times change almost from day to day, it is important to have this prayer timetable to be sure of the beginning and end of each prayer time.

In the example given on page 98 for 1 January in Melbourne, the Fajr prayer is held between 4.08 and 6.02 a.m. and the Zuhr prayer is between 1.24 and 5.17 p.m. In mosques, a prayer in congregation is held just after the commencement of the prayer time. For instance, in almost all mosques in Melbourne, a Fajr prayer in congregation will be held just after 4.08 a.m. on 1 January. In Australian mosques, only a few people would turn up for the dawn, noon and afternoon prayers, while many more would come to the mosque after work for their sunset and evening prayers. Those living close to the mosque would normally come to perform their prayer in congregation, but others would pray at home or at work.

There are several Internet sites which publish prayer times

Prayer Timetable: Melbourne

JANUARY

Date	Fajr Dawn	Shuruq Sunrise	Zuhr Noon	Asr Afternoon	Maghrib Sunset	Isha Evening
1	4:08	6:02	1:24	5:17	8:48	10:32
2	4:09	6:02	1:24	5:18	8:49	10:31
3	4:10	6:03	1:25	5:18	8:49	10:31
4	4:11	6:04	1:25	5:19	8:49	10:31
5	4:12	6:05	1:26	5:19	8:49	10:31
6	4:13	6:06	1:26	5:19	8:49	10:31
7	4:14	6:07	1:26	5:20	8:49	10:30

for the whole year in each capital city in Australia. Some newspapers such as *The Age* also publish Muslim prayer times. For those who are interested in having prayer times on their laptop or notebook, software is available to calculate prayer times anywhere in the world.

The following are special days in the Islamic calendar.

First of Muharram: Islamic new year

Usually in Muslim-majority countries, the first day of Muharram is a public holiday even though it is not a formal religious celebration. This is similar to Australians taking the first day of January off as a holiday. Australian Muslims do not generally celebrate the Islamic New Year. Some mosques and Islamic societies may organise a talk at the mosque or Islamic centre, but usually the day passes unnoticed for many Australian Muslims. Even in Muslim-majority countries where this day is an official holiday, there are no particular celebratory activities. The practices associated with New Year's Eve in Australia to welcome the new year are not part of the Muslim new year.

Twelfth of Rabi' al-Awwal: Birthday of the Prophet Muhammad

This date is believed to be the birthday of the Prophet Muhammad. Again, while it is not a religious event, many Muslims mark this day in celebration of the special place that the Prophet Muhammad has in their hearts. Usually, in Australia, Islamic centres and mosques organise special events, such as religious talks, barbecues, lunches or dinners at their premises to celebrate the day. Students at Islamic schools also will mark the day with special activities related to the day. If the date falls on a working day, the celebration remains a low-key event for many Muslims. Any activities will be after hours or postponed until the weekend.

Riyad Asvat

Celebration of the birthday of the Prophet

The celebration of the birthday of the Prophet I attended in June 2001 at a community hall in Hallam, Victoria, was indeed a memorable occasion for me. It was organised by the Shadhili *tariqa* (mystical order). There were approximately 200 people there. The males were segregated from the females by being accommodated at the front of the hall. The program began with the recitation of the Qur'an. The *hafidh* then recited the translation of the verses in English.

The followers of the Shadhili mystical order recited the prayers of the Moroccan Sufi master Shaykh Muhammad ibn al-Habib. The Pakistani followers of the Chishti order then sang the famous poem of Shaykh Sharaf al-din al-Busayri. This remarkable poem deals with the character and qualities of the Prophet Muhammad, may Allah bless him and grant him peace.

After the afternoon congregational prayer there was a talk by the Australian representative of the Shadhili master Shaykh Abdalqadir al-Sufi. He explained that the birthday of the Prophet celebrations were unique opportunities to recall the tremendous spiritual, political, economic and social legacy of the Prophet.

Then came the most delightful part of the afternoon, the contribution of the Ethiopian followers of the Rifa'i mystical order. A young lady from among them outlined the permissibility of celebrating the birth of the Prophet in Islamic law. She advised the gathering not to be distracted by attacks of fundamentalist and modernist Muslims against such occasions. The beautiful singing of the men, accompanied by their drums, followed the talk.

The program was brought to an end by the Fiji followers of the Qadiri mystical order who led the gathering in singing the salutations on the Prophet.

Twelfth of Rajab: Mi'raj al-Nabiy: 'Ascension' of the Prophet to heaven

Many Muslims commemorate the night that the Prophet Muhammad is believed to have 'ascended' to heaven and received instructions for the five daily prayers. For many Muslims, this 'ascension' was a spiritual journey, while others believe it was a physical one, in the sense that the Prophet was physically taken to the heavens and then returned to his home on the same night.

Month of Ramadan and the 'night of power'

Ramadan is the most sacred month of the year, during which Muslims fast every day of the month from dawn to sunset. In fact, the most sacred and celebrated night of the year occurs also during the month of Ramadan, somewhere in the final ten days.

It was during Ramadan that the Prophet Muhammad first began to receive qur'anic revelations. Muslims believe that on one of the odd days of the last ten days of Ramadan (21, 23, 25, 27 or 29), usually understood as the 27th, a special time called the 'night of power', or 'Laylat al-Qadr', occurs. The Qur'an refers to this night as being better than a thousand months. During Ramadan, devout Muslims will pray and recite the Qur'an as much as possible.

Festivities of Eid

Eid al-Fitr occurs immediately after the month of Ramadan on the First of Shawwal. Eid al-Ad ha occurs during the pilgrimage season, on the tenth of Dhu al-Hijja. Khurram Murad, a British Muslim, explains how Muslims approach the festivities of Eid:

> As Eid approaches, joyful expectations increase, the day is more talked of. Houses are cleaned and decorated, especially on the day and night before. New clothes are prepared, for everyone must wear his best. Near sunset all turn their eyes to the horizon—in corners, in open grounds. Some exchange cards and gifts—a recent addition. There is no selfish spending spree though; Eid is not a commercial venture. Delicious meals are cooked and, in sharing, heartily eaten. But not a morsel should be thrown away. Every worldly thing is from God, a bounty, and must therefore be made use of to honour His occasion, to rejoice in His greatest bounty. It is this spirit which pervades Eid celebrations. What does Eid celebrate again and again? God's bounty and His mercy.[1]

Australian Muslims, like others all over the world, celebrate Eid with much fanfare. On the Eid day, there is the Eid prayer after sunrise, which all Muslims (men, women, children) go to pray. The prayer is usually held in an open space such as a park, weather permitting, or in large mosques throughout the city. Relatives and friends then visit each other, give gifts to children, wear their best clothes, and take part in the festivities of the day. It is supposed to be a happy day for all, in which the rich give to the poor. It is a day of sharing. In Australia, if the Eid falls on a working day during the week, the Eid prayer is performed on that day in the morning and celebrations are postponed until the weekend. Some Muslims seek leave from work on that day,

Waleed: Celebrating Eid

When I think about how my extended family in Egypt would see my immediate family's celebration of Eid, I find it amusing to think of the confusion it would cause them. Rather than the proliferation of rich Middle Eastern food, we seem to prefer a barbecue after some backyard cricket with my nephews (and perhaps some football). My parents really have no choice—my brother and I simply take control, and it's amazing the influence a couple of toddlers can have. Sure, the traditional biscuits make an appearance (more for the purpose of making them than eating them) to provide the cultural bridge, but I can honestly say that Eid in this country, at least for our family, is quite unique.

But unquestionably, the day is about my nephews (Yusuf and Luqman), and their presents. All the games, all the food, it's all just build-up to the present-opening climax of the day, when hours of care in wrapping expensive parcels are ruined within a matter of seconds.

but many others continue working as if it is another normal working day.

In Melbourne, to celebrate Eid, Muslims from a variety of ethnic backgrounds get together in various parks for barbecues with family and friends. In the northern suburbs of Melbourne where there is a high concentration of Muslims, particularly Turkish, Muslims organise celebration of Eid in one or more parks. There is a carnival atmosphere, with stalls selling a variety of goods, from Islamic dress to books and videos, and all sorts of food items, such as Turkish kebabs, Indian tandoori chicken and Lebanese sweets. Rides for the children—including camel rides—are often provided. Muslims wearing new clothes, the old wearing the traditional clothes of their 'home country', and the young in the latest trendy clothes, provide a contrast between the old and the young. Some women wear the scarf, or hijab; others may wear tight jeans and T-shirts. The contrasts point to the community's mix of people in terms of their adherence to the traditional Islamic dress codes. Turkish, Arabic or Indian music is played. Bargain hunters may seek out Islamic clothes, posters, books or prayer mats. An Eid festival is the place to see the diversity of Islam in all its real-life aspects: ethnic, cultural, religious and generational. The celebrations may continue over a whole weekend. Local politicians are often invited to give talks in the official part of these celebrations.

Friday prayers

Muslims do not have a Sabbath, as do Jews; however, once a week, on Fridays, Muslims gather together at around noon for special congregational prayers. While the five daily prayers can be performed individually anywhere—at home, at work or else-where—the Friday prayer has to be performed in congregation. The Friday prayer replaces the Zuhr prayer for the day, and there is a sermon before the actual prayer. For this, one has to go to a mosque. Australian Muslims do try to arrange an hour or so off work to perform this obligatory duty, and usually employers are sympathetic to such requests. Given that it falls in the lunch break, getting this time off is not usually a problem. In some prayer facilities, such as those on university campuses, Friday prayer is held during the lunch break between 1 and 2 p.m. to allow for students, staff and others to attend the prayer without taking additional time off.

Once the 'call to prayer' is completed, the imam gives a sermon of two parts. The sermon is usually about an issue of concern to the Muslims of the local community at the time, but it always includes exhortations regarding the importance of following the religion. If the mosque is located in a predominantly Turkish area, such as the Thomastown mosque in the northern suburbs of Melbourne, and is led by a Turkish imam, then the sermon is usually in Turkish. If it is located in a predominantly Arab area (say, Lebanese), it is in Arabic. In mosques where those who come to pray are from a variety of ethnic backgrounds and the mosque is not controlled by one ethnic group, the sermon is usually in English—for instance, the Islamic Council of Victoria mosque in the city of Melbourne, where mostly professionals working in the city area come to pray. In some mosques, part of the sermon is given in English. Or, when the imam completes his sermon in the ethnic language, an interpreter may provide a summarised version of it in English. Given the multi-ethnic nature of the student/staff population at Australian universities, and the fact that universities do not have a specific imam, English is used for the Friday sermon on university campuses, where students and staff take it in turns to lead the prayer throughout the year.

SACRED PLACES IN ISLAM

All groups of people have places that are very important to them. At the heart of Australia, Uluru has been special to Aboriginal people since time immemorial. Elsewhere, Australians have built Remembrance memorials for those who died fighting in the great World Wars, and the Great Barrier Reef is protected as one of the natural wonders of the world. Muslims also have special places, some of which are considered blessed by God, and others have great religious significance.

Mecca and Medina

For a Muslim, Mecca in present-day Saudi Arabia is the most sacred city on earth. Muslims from around the world, including Australia, turn towards Mecca at least five times a day when they pray. The most sacred place in Mecca is the Ka'ba and the surrounding Grand Mosque. Only Muslims are allowed to enter Mecca.

The next most important sacred place for Muslims is Medina, the city of the Prophet. The first mosque in Islam was built there in a place called Quba, today a suburb of modern Medina. The second mosque built in Medina is called 'Mosque of the Prophet' where the Prophet Muhammad and the first two caliphs (political successors to the Prophet) are buried. It is also in Medina that graves of several of the Prophet Muhammad's closest companions lie. Like Mecca, only Muslims are allowed to enter Medina. Non-Muslims visiting areas close to the cities of Mecca and Medina are required to stay in hotels located outside the city limits, or to drive around the perimeter on specially marked roads.

Jerusalem

The third most sacred place in Islam is Jerusalem, because of its connection to the earlier prophets. Moreover, Jerusalem is believed to be the place where the Prophet Muhammad miraculously travelled to and then 'ascended' to the heavens in his 'night journey'. The Qur'an refers to the destination of the Prophet on this journey as 'the Remote House of Worship', or al-Masjid al-Aqsa. It was much later, after the death of the Prophet Muhammad, that the Aqsa Mosque was built, as well as the famous 'Dome of the Rock', to mark the area's special significance. The Dome of the Rock, built in Jerusalem by the Umayyad caliph Abd al-Malik and completed in 691, is the earliest extant Islamic monument.

Although many Muslims think that Jerusalem is sacred because of these monuments, its real symbolic importance lies in the belief that Jerusalem is the place where God's connection to the created world occurred through the agency of prophethood.

Karbala

For Shi'i Muslims, Karbala in Iraq is one of the holiest places, being the place where the third Shi'i imam and the Prophet's grandson, Husayn, is buried. Karbala is situated on the bank of the river Euphrates, 50 kilometres southeast of Baghdad. It was here that, in 681, Husayn and his small army, including his brothers, sisters, sons and daughters, fought against the Umayyad army sent to pressure them to pay allegiance to the Umayyad caliph and submit to the caliph's authority. In this battle, Husayn and many of his family members and associates were killed. The battle at Karbala is now remembered during the first ten days of the month of Muharram (the first month of the Islamic calander) by Shi'is. Many Australian Muslims of Shi'i background visit Karbala.

Shrines of 'holy' figures

Apart from these places and general places of worship, at a popular level many Muslims visit the tombs and shrines of so-called holy figures. It is hoped that visiting the resting place of a mystic or scholar (*shaykh*) might lead the shaykh to intercede with God on the pilgrim's behalf. The importance of a particular shrine may be associated with the local culture, or it may draw visitors from around the world. Such tombs and shrines, which are often associated with a mosque and beautifully decorated, play an important part in the social and religious life of their communities. However, there are many Muslims who believe that the practice of visiting tombs is highly discouraged, if not prohibited, in Islam. Given the rather recent history of Islam in Australia, there are no such shrines of 'holy' figures in Australia. Often Australian Muslims tend to go back to their countries of origin to visit such shrines.

The mosque (masjid)

One of the most common of special places to a Muslim is the mosque. The word 'masjid' means 'place of prostration', or the place where daily prayers are conducted. Wherever Muslims live, a mosque or a prayer faciltity is normally found. Although the notion of a mosque as a separate building has taken deep root in Muslim communities, a mosque does not necessarily have to be a building. In Islam, any clean place may be used for worship, even parks and other open spaces. In one sense, when the time for prayer occurs, any clean place that Muslims find themselves in may become a place of worship. The Prophet reportedly said, 'The earth is a masjid for you. So pray wherever you are at the time of prayer.' However, it is true that, from the very beginning, Muslims began to build structures that were specially set aside for worship and other religious activities. The Prophet himself established at least two mosques in Medina, and even before that, the area surrounding the Ka'ba in Mecca was considered a mosque.

A mosque is more than a place of worship. It is a place for prayer, study and even social interaction among friends. In Australia it is a place where new arrivals often go to meet local people in the Muslim community. There are three different types of mosques in Australia: a mosque with several facilities, such as classrooms, a bookshop and offices; a mosque with no such facilities; and prayer rooms, such as those on many university campuses. Some mosques were originally churches that were purchased by Muslims and then converted to mosques. Since a church is a place of religious worship, often the problems associated with permission from the local council to establish or build a mosque can be avoided simply by buying an existing church.

A mosque can be anything from a simple building to a large, highly decorated structure with a tall minaret. The architecture of mosques varies from culture to culture, but there are some basic features common to most mosques. These include a prayer hall, a pulpit (*minbar*), an open courtyard, a dome of some kind, and a minaret. Usually in Muslim-majority countries, the call to prayer is made from the minaret five times a day using loud-speakers. In Australia, because of council regulations, the minaret is not used for this purpose but it exists as part of the mosque architecture.

There are separate prayer areas for men and women. If the mosque has two storeys, usually the ground floor is for men and the upper floor for women. In some mosques, the hall is divided into two sections: one for men, the other for women. In some mosques, there is a partition between these sections. Separate facilities for men and women will be set aside for the ritual washing of the hands, face, arms and feet before prayer.

A small curved niche in the front wall of the mosque indicates the direction of Mecca. In larger mosques, there are separate facilities for classrooms. In smaller mosques, classes are held in the prayer hall and participants sit on the floor. No chairs or desks are used in the prayer hall.

No images of living beings are used in mosques. Muslims believe that God cannot be represented in any form; such a representation is considered blasphemous in Islam. Muslims also do not use images of the Prophet or, for that matter, any other prophet such as Moses or Jesus. Any decoration of the mosque is usually with verses from the Qur'an written in a highly ornamental style, or with the names of God, or that of the Prophet and senior companions of the Prophet, written in Arabic. Apart from geometrical patterns, calligraphy is mostly used for decoration purposes.

In Australia, the first prayer facilities for Muslims were established by the early Afghan settlers in the late 1800s. Two mosques were built in Coolgardie which, in 1898, was the main Muslim settlement of the time. The buildings and rooms set aside for prayer provided minimal services, simply because the community was so small and scattered. By the 1950s, the building of permanent mosques began in a slow and determined fashion. Prayer facilities were established in various parts of Sydney, Melbourne, Adelaide and Perth, which led to the building of more permanent mosques in all the capital cities.

In the 1970s, governments and wealthy individuals in oil-producing countries such as Saudi Arabia, the United Arab Emirates, Kuwait and Libya donated substantial funds to Muslim minorities living in the West, including Australia. This resulted in a significant increase in mosque-building activities from the late 1970s and continuing today. There was no central body directing the building of mosques in Australia. Local communities often approached contacts overseas, either in the Middle East or in their home countries. Turkey, for instance, provided funds for establishing community centres and mosques in Australia, as well as providing religious leaders to serve the local Turkish Muslim community. The Broadmeadows Mosque in Melbourne and the Auburn Mosque in Sydney, for example, were both constructed with local collections and some help from the Turkish government. At the time of writing, there are more than 100 mosques in Australia, most of them in Sydney and Melbourne. In addition, a large number of prayer facilities exist

Auburn Gallipoli Mosque, Sydney[2]

The mosque stands on a site measuring one acre, or 4000 square metres. The construction of the current mosque began on 23 November 1986. It was officially opened on 28 November 1999. It took a painstaking thirteen years to complete, due to the time needed to raise funds through donations.

Omer Kirazoglu is the architect of the mosque. The same design is used in Turkey at a number of places, such as Istanbul University's Faculty of Theology. The marble and stone used on the external walls and in the courtyard were imported from Turkey. Its carpet was manufactured in Istanbul and is especially designed for mosque use. There are 25 crystal chandeliers that were also manufactured in Istanbul. Three doors of the mosque are designed and produced in the classical Ottoman style. The wood of the doors is from special trees and the doors are produced without using nails. In 1993, the internal calligraphy and embroidery of the mosque were designed by the calligrapher Huseyin Oksuz and painted by a team of five artists in five-and-a-half months.

on university campuses and in Muslim community centres. Mosques in Australia are often managed by an association responsible for both the operation of the mosque and the affairs of the local Muslim community.

Mosques are established not only for religious reasons, but also for linguistic and cultural purposes. In Turkish mosques, for instance, children may receive instruction in the Turkish language, as well as religious training. In Indo-Pakistani mosques, it is the Urdu language, among others, which is used by the community. Thus, mosques and community centres are a means for preserving an ethnic group's linguistic and cultural, as well as religious, identity.

Chapter 8

LIVING AS AN AUSTRALIAN PRACTISING MUSLIM

Like other faiths, Islam places emphasis on proper conduct in almost all areas of life. Guidelines for this are provided by what is referred to as Islamic law and ethics. A significant part of this applies to Muslims in Australia, as it applies to Muslims elsewhere, but a large part of traditional Islamic law is not applicable, as Muslims are a minority group subject to Australian law as are all other Australians. Examples of non-applicable laws include Islamic criminal law (for example, punishments related to adultery, theft and murder), Islamic contract law, and the Islamic law of peace and war. Instead, Muslims follow Australian law in these areas.

Much of what Australian Muslims practise as Islamic law is related to various rituals, certain aspects of family law to the extent that Australian law permits (such as in the case of marriage), and to what Muslims can practise as individuals in their own personal life, such as avoiding gambling, prostitution, sex outside marriage, and so on. Other examples include Islamic dietary laws (such as the avoidance of alcohol and other intoxicants), Islamic norms of dress, Islamic ethics related to earning a living, recreation, social relations, and those related to the parent–child relationship. In observing these norms, the practising Muslim fulfils the requirements of the law in his or her personal life.

Understanding Islamic law and ethics

Law in Islam is understood in fairly broad terms; it deals with a person's moral and ethical conduct, their religious duties (such as prayer), as well as standard areas of the law, such as property, family, contract and international law. Islamic law is generally referred to as *shari'a law*, or just shari'a.

Under Islamic law, all actions of a Muslim are classified into five categories:

- *Obligatory:* an action that *must* be performed by a Muslim—for example, the five daily prayers.
- *Recommended:* an action that is not considered obligatory but is highly recommended—for example, brushing one's teeth before performing a prayer.
- *Reprehensible:* an action that is not prohibited but is preferably avoided. An example of this is fasting continuously for consecutive days, without eating or drinking at all.
- *Prohibited:* an action that *must not* be performed by a Muslim—for example, stealing.

- *Permitted:* any action that does not fall into any of the above four categories. The vast majority of human activity falls into this category, such as walking, using a computer, playing football, talking, and so on.

These five categories play an important role in a practising Muslim's life, which means that in their day-to-day living, a practising Australian Muslim is conscious of the importance of his or her actions and attempts to follow Islamic norms and practices to the extent possible under Australian law.

JUDGING THE PERMITTED AND THE PROHIBITED: THE SOURCES

In order to answer the question, 'How does a Muslim know whether an action falls into any one of the five categories?', it is important to know that there are two fundamental authorities in Islam: the authority of God and the authority of the Prophet Muhammad. The authority of God is the most important one and is represented in the Muslim holy scripture, the Qur'an, which Muslims believe is the direct word of God. The authority of the Prophet is represented in 'the traditions of the Prophet' known as *hadith* (or *sunna*), which are the sayings and deeds of the Prophet Muhammad.

The Qur'an

The Qur'an is essentially a collection of revelations that the Prophet Muhammad received over a 23-year period. It is now in the form of a book more or less the size of the Bible, with

114 chapters (sura) of unequal length. The Qur'an covers many things:

- It talks about God and His message to humanity.
- It discusses ethical and moral issues, such as injustice in the community and the need to help the disadvantaged.
- It instructs Muslims to behave in certain ways in certain circumstances.
- It talks about past prophets such as Adam, Noah, Abraham, Ishmael, Isaac, Joseph, Moses and Jesus, among others.
- It narrates the stories of these prophets and their people, including the messages they taught.
- It narrates some stories of the Prophet Muhammad's own mission and struggles.
- It elaborates on what happens after death.
- It talks about the creation of the universe.

The Qur'an is an unusual book in the sense that it does not deal with one topic in a given chapter. It moves from topic to topic, and to understand it one needs a basic understanding of the life of the Prophet and the history of the first Muslim community (during the period 610–632).

For Muslims, the Qur'an is literally the word of God, not the words or opinions of Muhammad. The revelations were, for the most part, written down during the lifetime of the Prophet and collected in book form shortly after his passing—that is, within two years of the Prophet's death. Interestingly, the revelations are not arranged in chronological order. The first revelation, for instance, is not the first section of the Qur'an in its present form. Instead, the chapters are organised roughly in order of longest to shortest, with the exception of the first chapter, which is the central prayer of Islam. Recited many times during the day by Muslims, the first chaper reads:

> *In the name of God, the Most Gracious, the Dispenser of Grace:*
> *All praise is due to God alone, the Sustainer of all the worlds,*
> *The Most Gracious, the Dispenser of Grace,*
> *Lord of the Day of Judgment!*
> *Thee alone do we worship; and unto Thee alone do we turn for aid.*
> *Guide us the straight way—*
> *The way of those upon whom Thou hast bestowed Thy blessings,*
> *Not of those who have been condemned [by Thee],*
> *Nor of those who go astray!*

Because, for a Muslim, the Qur'an is God's word, its instructions, commands and prohibitions are to be followed. For instance, the Qur'an forbids, among other things:

- Adultery: 'do not commit adultery—for, behold, it is an abomination and an evil way' (17:32).
- Eating certain foods: 'forbidden to you is carrion, and blood, and the flesh of swine, and that over which any name other than God's has been invoked . . . ' (5:3).
- Backbiting and slander: 'woe unto every slanderer, fault-finder' (104:1).

Muslims believe that there is no other authority in Islam that can challenge these commands of God, for example, by saying that it is morally permissible to commit adultery.

Hadith

Next to the authority of God is the authority of the Prophet Muhammad. The Prophet explained what the Qur'an meant and put qur'anic instructions into practice. A good example of this is prayer. The Qur'an commands Muslims to perform daily prayers, but it does not give any details as to how, when and what form these prayers should take. The Prophet Muhammad explained prayer in detail and showed Muslims how to perform it. For Muslims, it is essential to learn about what the Prophet taught, said and did in order to practise Islam in their daily life.

Traditions about the life of the Prophet are known as hadith. They are the recollections of individuals who lived with the Prophet and who later reported things the Prophet said and did, what he approved of, and other information about him.

In the first 300 years of Islam, hadith collectors travelled across the Islamic world, studying with prominent scholars of hadith, collecting and writing them down, determining which hadith were reliable and which were fabricated and had been wrongly attributed to the Prophet. In the process, these hadith scholars compiled many volumes that list what they considered to be reliable hadith. Some of the most famous collections are those by the Sunni scholars, Bukhari and Muslim, and the Shi'i scholar, Kulayni.

Both the Qur'an and the collections of hadith are written in Arabic. For those who cannot read Arabic, translations are available in many languages, including English.

INTERPRETING ISLAMIC LAW

Not all of the possible actions of a Muslim's daily life are spelled out clearly in the Qur'an and the traditions of the Prophet. It is not possible for any text to list and identify every conceivable action of a person, let alone all people or all Muslims. What this means is that, throughout history, there developed a need to relate the Qur'an and the traditions of the Prophet to the situations in which Muslims found themselves. Both the Qur'an and the traditions of the Prophet provided guidelines for Muslims by providing a basis for understanding what actions and deeds could be considered prohibited or permitted. For example, there is nothing in the Qur'an or the traditions about watching television or eating Vegemite. Thus, in order to understand what Islam has to say on these and similar issues, Muslims turn to scholars (or experts in Islamic law).

Scholars who have studied the Qur'an, the traditions of the Prophet, the history and development of Islam, as well as other disciplines necessary for understanding Islam, have a special role in interpreting the foundational texts for Muslims in each generation. A scholar can be a man or a woman.

Such scholars existed right from the very beginning of Islam. Following the Prophet, key figures in early Muslim history, such as his wife Ayesha, taught others about Islam. Today, scholars in Islam exist in all Muslim communities, including Australia. The role of scholars is to interpret the foundational texts and to relate them to the changing needs of Muslims throughout the world. These scholars often work individually and their works are circulated and debated. Some of their views may be accepted, while others may be rejected by the broader Muslim community.

GENERAL PRINCIPLES IN ISLAMIC LAW AND ETHICS

Some general principles exist in Islam to make it easier for people to determine how to act in their daily life and how to practise their religion:

- All things are permissible for a Muslim except those things that are clearly prohibited in the Qur'an and the traditions of the Prophet. Consequently, out of the vast majority of human activities, only a very small number of things are actually prohibited in Islam.

- What is prohibited in the Qur'an or in the traditions of the Prophet cannot be made permissible in Islam by any Muslim. For example, the Qur'an says that gambling is prohibited, and as such no Muslim has the authority to make it permissible for Muslims.

- What is permitted clearly in the Qur'an or in the traditions of the Prophet cannot be made prohibited. For example, the Qur'an says that fish is a permissible type of food; therefore no Muslim may declare that eating fish is morally reprehensible and forbidden.

- In cases of necessity, prohibited things may become permissible for the duration of a need. For instance, if a person finds himself in a place where there is nothing to eat at all except pork, he may eat it rather than starve to death, even though pork is normally prohibited to a Muslim.

In addition to these basic principles related to law, there are several general principles related to Islamic ethics, which guide Islamic morals and manners. For example, a Muslim is expected to:

- treat others as he or she would wish them to treat him or her;
- not ask a person to do something which he/she would not do himself or herself;
- avoid acts that may harm himself or herself or others;
- be gentle, courteous and kind in dealing with others;
- observe the values of elegance, beauty and orderliness in all that he or she does;
- observe silence if there is nothing useful to say—that is, one should avoid unnecessary speech;
- observe cleanliness of one's body, clothes and residence;
- not be hasty in making decisions;
- be moderate in his or her views and approaches and avoid taking extreme positions;
- be generous and not be mean or stingy;
- be self-sufficient, and seek help from others (even from the government, such as social security payments) only when it is absolutely essential;
- earn one's livelihood and not be dependent on others (including the government) to provide this;
- be disciplined in one's life;
- be tolerant of other people and their views, even though he or she may not agree with them;
- not be extravagant (for example, in one's spending); and
- be respectful towards others—in particular, parents and elders.

Of course, not all Muslims put these ethical norms into practice, but devout Muslims attempt to put into practice as many of them as possible.

Examples of things prohibited in Islam

Food and drinks: meat of an animal that dies of natural causes; pork; pig-based products; blood; alcoholic beverages, including beer and wine.

Earning a livelihood: cheating; stealing; misappropriation; prostitution; manufacturing and trading in alcoholic beverages and drugs; hoarding; price manipulation; fraud; bribery; exploitation; trading in stolen property; usury; gambling.

Morality: backbiting; slandering; defamation; insulting parents; sex outside marriage.

Marriage of a man with his: mother; step-mother; grandmother; daughter; grand-daughter; sister; paternal or maternal aunt; niece; foster mother; foster sister; mother-in-law; step-daughter; daughter-in-law; a married woman.

Marriage of a woman with her: father; step-father; grandfather; son; grandson; brother; paternal or maternal uncle; nephew; foster father; foster brother; father-in-law; step-son; son-in-law.

A cursory look at the examples given in the boxed text reveals that there is a lot of similarity between what is unacceptable in Islam and what is considered unacceptable in Australia.

There is a view among some Muslims, as well as non-Muslims, that in order to function as a Muslim, a person has to live in a 'Muslim' society (or in a Muslim-majority country where Islamic law is implemented). This is not entirely valid, for a variety of reasons. More than 30 per cent of Muslims in the world live in countries with centuries-long established minority Muslim communities, such as India, Russia and China, and other parts of Asia and Africa. Although there may be certain constraints, generally speaking, those who want to live an 'Islamic' life are able to do so in these countries.

The fact that certain things that are prohibited for a Muslim are allowed in non-Muslim-majority societies does not mean that a Muslim has to partake of them. For instance, alcohol is easily available in Australia; however, practising Muslims do not suddenly find they have an urge to drink just because alcohol is available. And a practising Muslim living in Australia would not take up gambling even if he lived next-door to a casino. Thus, following Islamic norms becomes a function of a person's individual commitment to the religion, without the need for 'religious police' to enforce Islamic norms in the society.

Many Muslims find that they experience little difficulty in living as practising Muslims in a country like Australia where there is religious freedom and no interference from the state in matters of belief, practice, and theological orientations of Muslims.

NEGOTIATING SOME AUSTRALIAN LAWS, NORMS AND PRACTICES

Nevertheless, for Muslims living in non-Muslim-majority countries like Australia, there can be some difficult areas that require adjustment and negotiation. Examples include:

Eating out

Because Islam requires Muslims to eat meat which is slaughtered according to Islamic guidelines (known as halal meat), many practising Muslims would not go to restaurants and food outlets that do not serve such meat. Similarly, they would avoid places where ham and pork are served. Given that alcohol is prohibited, they also would avoid bars. This may limit some aspects of entertainment for a practising Muslim. However, today in Australia, an increasing number of halal food outlets, including restaurants, are open for business. Even some fast-food chains have opened halal outlets in suburbs where a large Muslim population exists. Given the similarity between food regulations in Jewish law and Islamic law, Muslims may often go to *kosher* food outlets if they cannot find a halal restaurant. To avoid the problem of meat, many may simply opt for a vegetarian or seafood dish.

Banking and interest

Many Muslims believe that interest is prohibited in Islam—that is, that one should not pay or accept interest. Since Australian financial institutions charge and pay interest, some practising Muslims are likely to avoid conventional banks if they are able to do so. But for the vast majority of Muslims, avoiding banking institutions is not an option, even though they may believe that interest is prohibited in Islam. In order to avoid accepting any interest, some practising Muslims request their bank not to credit any interest to their accounts. Some other Muslims may accept the interest but give it to a charity. These Muslims would also avoid, as much as possible, entering into transactions which may require them to pay interest. Thus, for instance, they will take advantage of credit card facilities in which there is an interest-free period and will pay their account during this period. Nevertheless, if there is no option but to pay, as in the case of home mortgages, such practising Muslims will reluctantly contract interest-bearing loans, given that Islamic law allows one to engage in practices that are prohibited under Islamic law if one is compelled to do so or in the case of dire necessity. Buying a home, for example, is considered such a necessity. There are also many Muslims who do not consider that interest is prohibited. For them, therefore, dealing with banks and interest poses no problem.

In order to deal with the problem of avoiding interest, a Muslim financial institution, the Muslim Community Co-operative of Australia, that is based on profit and loss sharing, not interest, has been established in Australia. A small number of Muslims are members of this cooperative.

Divorce

Under Islamic law, if there are irreconcilable differences in a marriage, a husband and wife may choose to divorce. The laws related to divorce in Islamic law are somewhat different to those in Australian law, however. For example, in Islam there is no requirement for a period of separation before divorce. Since Australian law does not recognise Islamic divorce laws, a practising Muslim may have some difficulties in this area. Generally speaking, Muslims tend to adjust to the situation by following both Australian law as well as the Islamic requirements for divorce. At times this can be difficult, but the problem is manageable.

Prayer

A Muslim is required to pray five times a day: at dawn, noon, afternoon, sunset and night. Children at school, and those who are working standard hours of nine to five, may find it difficult to pray the noon or afternoon prayer. But this is also manageable, since most people can organise to pray during their breaks. The prayer, which only takes a few minutes, can be performed anywhere that is clean, such as a classroom or a work office.

 ## Yasmin: Working and the Muslim prayer

I approached my interview, as most people do, with the usual accompaniment of butterflies in the stomach. With me, however, it felt more like a swarm of bees. I wasn't sure if this was because I was nervous about the interview or because I feared the reaction of the interviewers because I was an Australian woman who was Muslim.

The interview went well and I felt confident that I did my best. A couple of weeks later I got the call I was hoping for. I got the job!

I started work and initially it was groundbreaking, because a Muslim had never been employed in my department before.

Most of the people had never worked with or known any Muslims. People tend either to treat you like everyone else or to ignore you because they don't know how to behave around you. Within a few weeks, after people realise you are a 'normal person', everything falls into place. My occupation is very much client-based, and people are comfortable to deal with me on the phone. The initial meeting is one of surprise! I often wonder how people construct their perceptions of Muslim women, because most people are shocked that one can be educated and work as part of a professional organisation.

In terms of prayer, which is obligatory for Muslims, I use a small room off my office and close the door. Everyone knows that I am praying and this has become a normal part of our office routine. If the phone rings or someone is looking for me, my colleagues say I'm praying and will be finished soon. The period between prayers is long enough for me to be able to juggle my obligations to God and those to my employer. I work in a very flexible environment. If we are on the road conducting training sessions or attending meetings or workshops and it's time to pray, I either occupy a small area at the back, or perhaps during lunch I request a small private place. People see that I am comfortable with my faith and often approach me later with a barrage of questions which I am only too happy to answer.

The Australian work culture has been described as a 'beer culture'. Friday drinks at the pub are off-limits for me, so I excuse myself. It came to the attention of my colleagues that this was a regular pattern and when I was asked why, I told them it wasn't appropriate for me to be in pubs or around people drinking alcohol. I never asked for 'special' treatment, but a lot of people said they didn't really like drinking either, so we rotate venues so that everyone can be included.

Muslims are people like everyone else, and even though women in particular may appear different, it doesn't take long to realise that we have many things in common with others: moral values, hobbies, favourite recipes, sports and novels. Since commencing work in my occupation I believe I have enhanced the lives of others greatly, just as they have enhanced mine. It was a great lesson for all of us. Don't judge a book by its cover! That's my challenge for you!

ISLAMIC CRIMINAL LAW AND AUSTRALIAN MUSLIMS

One of the key areas of interest in Australia is Islamic criminal law and its punishments. Many Australians wonder why Islam still clings to what they consider to be 'mediaeval' or 'barbaric' forms of punishment, such as capital punishment for murder, flogging for unlawful sex and amputation of the hand for theft. This issue comes up every time there is a debate in Australia on an issue related to Islamic law, or when an Australian or a European is involved in a high-profile case involving one of these crimes in an Islamic country where Islamic criminal law is applied, such as Saudi Arabia. For instance, in the case of Yvonne Gilford, the Australian nurse murdered in Saudi Arabia in 1996, the media spotlight was on the Islamic law of 'blood money', which in the case of murder is a payment made by the family of the murderer to the family of the victim. Because Yvonne's brother Frank was willing to accept the blood money, there was much outrage in the Australian media about his decision. Islamic law as it exists in Saudi Arabia was labelled at the time as mediaeval, barbaric, and so on.

Islamic criminal law and its punishments exist in classical Islamic legal texts. For murder, Islamic law gives three options to the victim's family: demand capital punishment from the court; accept blood money; or forgive the murderer. The choice is for the victim's family to make. In the case of unlawful sex, Islamic law specifies flogging of both parties. However, the evidential requirements for proving guilt are, in most cases, almost impossible to meet. For example, four witnesses must have seen the parties engaging in sexual intercourse. Similarly, for amputation for theft, there are many conditions that have to be met before the amputation is carried out. A poor person who steals to feed his hungry family or himself, or someone found guilty of a minor theft offence, will not be punished with amputation of a hand. In fact, even the classical Islamic legal texts have laid out so many conditions to be met before any of these harsh punishments can be carried out that, in practice, carrying out these punishments becomes, in many cases, almost impossible. Thus, the importance of these punishments often lies in their symbolic deterrence value. Those Muslims who argue in favour of these punishments today would point out the safety and security enjoyed by countries such as Saudi Arabia where cases of theft, burglary, assault and murder are few compared to those countries which do not implement such harsh punishments.

Whatever the merits or demerits of these punishments, in the modern period, in only a very few Muslim countries (out of the more than 56 Muslim-majority countries) are these punishments still in place. The vast majority of Muslim countries have opted not to impose these punishments and instead use other forms of punishment such as fines or imprisonment. There is also a vigorous debate among Muslims on the necessity or importance of implementing these punishments. Some Muslims argue that in a Muslim-majority state, Islamic law, including its criminal law (as developed in classical Islamic law), must be implemented, along with these punishments. Many other Muslims, however, argue that what is important is not the implementation of the punishments but the avoidance of these 'crimes' or 'sins'. For them, the punishment is not itself an objective or an ideal.

In any case, the debate on these punishments in the context of Australia is irrelevant, as there are no calls among Australian Muslims to implement these punishments or to apply Islamic criminal law to Muslims. Even the most traditionalist Muslims do not entertain such ideas in Australia; even if some Muslims did, there is no possiblity that such calls would be listened to in Australia.

Chapter 9

MUSLIM COMMUNITY LEADERSHIP

In Australia, several types and levels of leadership exist among Muslims, and so it is difficult to talk about the role of 'Muslim leader' in a generalised sense. It is, however, more useful to highlight different types of leaders and the roles they play in the community.

NON-CORPORATE LEADERSHIP

In the case of a mosque, where the building of the mosque has been the result of individual initiative, a person or a small group of people may assume leadership in terms of the running of the mosque and its associated activities, using collective decision making. People who are involved in this manner may not necessarily be religious 'leaders' as such. They could be lay people from the community—professionals such as accountants, lawyers, doctors, teachers, and so on—who are keen to establish a mosque and provide services to the local Muslim community. In fact, this form of leadership is very common throughout Australia and many mosques run along these lines. Some mosques are built using funds provided by a foreign government, such as from Turkey or Saudi Arabia, or through the assistance of a major overseas benefactor. In such cases, representatives working on behalf of the foreign government or benefactor may remain part of the mosque leadership. Other mosques are run by societies or associations with a constitution stipulating some sort of revolving leadership, thus preventing one person or group dominating the mosque or society.

The religious leader of the mosque, the imam, is the person engaged in the day-to-day running of the mosque and its activities. In Australia, an imam is roughly equivalent to a 'minister of religion'. According to the Australian Standard Classification of Occupations (ASCO), 'ministers of religion' perform spiritual functions associated with beliefs and practices of religious faiths and provide motivation, guidance and training in religious life for the people of a congregation, parish or community. The entry requirement for this unit group is a bachelor degree or higher qualification. There is a requirement for high levels of personal commitment and interest, as well as formal qualifications or experience.

The tasks of an imam include:

- conducting regular prayers (salat);
- preparing and delivering sermons (for instance, Fridays) and special talks;
- giving advice and spiritual direction;

- participating in the social and welfare activities of the community, encouraging people to be aware of their responsibilities, and organising participation in community projects;
- conducting classes of religious instruction, and supervising prayer and discussion groups;
- conducting premarital and family counselling and referring people to professional service agencies where necessary; and
- performing marriages and funerals according to religious and civil law and keeping records as required by law.

Profile of an imam

Sheikh Fehmi Naji al-Imam (known as 'Sheikh Fehmi') arrived in Melbourne in 1951 from Lebanon. He was 23 at the time. Since then he has been an active member of the Melbourne Muslim community. He was instrumental in establishing the first Islamic Society in Victoria in 1957. Sheikh Fehmi organised the first weekend school in Melbourne in 1957 with fifteen students to help children learn about Islam and their language, Arabic. With other leading members of the Muslim community, he played a major role in building the mosque-cum-Islamic centre in the Melbourne suburb of Preston, one of the largest mosques in Melbourne. He collected donations from the local community and approached overseas donors for the rest of the funds to complete the project. He remained the full-time imam of the mosque for more than 25 years. Sheikh Fehmi still retains a busy schedule in meetings and community-related activities. He is a marriage celebrant, teacher of religious education at the mosque, liaises with the government, and works with refugees and those in need in the community.

Sheikh Fehmi is one of the most active Muslim participants in the inter-faith dialogue, and one of the executive directors of the World Conference on Religion and Peace of Australia. He adopts a moderate interpretation of Islam and strongly believes that Muslims should live harmoniously in this multi-cultural Australia. For his work in this area, he received one of Australia's highest awards, the Order of Australia.[1]

In Australia, most imams are generally 'imported' from over-seas, where they will have been trained in religious disciplines. Many of the imams are graduates of Islamic seminaries in India, Pakistan or Indonesia, or of universities such as Azhar University in Egypt, or the Islamic University of Saudi Arabia.

If a mosque is run by a particular ethnic group—for instance, Turkish, Pakistani, Afghani, Egyptian or Iranian—the imam generally is also from that background and is brought to Australia from the 'home' country. Not all mosques are clearly divided along ethnic lines, however, and therefore the choice of imam can vary. In most cases, the dominant voices in the mosque leadership can usually convince others to bring over an imam from a community closely associated with themselves.

This type of imported religious leadership sometimes leads to certain problems, with some of the imams being unaware of local Australian culture and even lacking basic English language skills. The problem is less severe when the imam is in charge of a mosque largely serving a particular ethnic group, as both the imam and the worshippers would share the 'home' language and even subscribe to a similar religious outlook. However, linguistic and cultural discrepancies can create considerable problems, especially when it comes to converts or second- and third-generation Australian Muslims who may not speak the imam's language—whether Persian, Arabic, Turkish or otherwise—and may have significantly different perspectives and outlook. In this case, it can be difficult to keep lines of communication open between imported religious leaders and significant sections of the community.

Because of this, there is a growing feeling among Muslims that it is important to establish Australian institutions for the training of home-grown religious leaders. This is still an unrealised dream, as it will take some time for the community to develop programs of training, especially given the enormous amount of resources required for such a venture. This means that, in the immediate future, religious leaders in Australia will continue to be imported from overseas. It is only recently that we are beginning to see the emergence of some Australian-born Muslims who are travelling to Muslim countries such as Malaysia for their religious training, in order to return and play an important role in local community affairs. It is these Muslims, who speak English and are comfortable and familiar with the Australian environment, who can play an increasingly significant role in the life of the Australian Muslim community, but the number of such leaders is still small.

Emerging parallel to the overseas training of Australian-born Muslims is another type of religious authority, which can be referred to as 'lay' leadership. These are people who have not gone through formal traditional Islamic religious training, but who are well-read in the area of Islam or Islamic studies. Some have taken up the role of religious leaders, or imams (not necessarily full-time), in some mosques or Muslim communities and societies.

Aziz Cooper
Being a Muslim chaplain

As a chaplain, I am responsible for the spiritual well-being of prisoners, as well as counselling and advocacy on their behalf. Most have a pretty basic Islamic faith—they may not know a lot—and they need support from the Muslim community. To give you one example, recently I visited a Muslim in a fairly isolated prison that was difficult to get to, and when I arrived she was so overcome she started weeping because she was so happy that someone had taken the time to come and see her. She had thought the Muslim community had forgotten about her and felt lonely and isolated.

What keeps me going is seeing a prisoner meet Allah and say 'God I've blown it, I've really stuffed up my life, but I need a second chance', and when they really repent, Allah meets them and does something special in their life. One guy expresses his remorse through his art and has won several awards. Many prisoners are in denial though.

> Another part of my job is to advocate on behalf of the prisoners, liaising with the prison staff. Things that seem little can become big issues, like when dogs are used to sniff around religious items like Qur'ans and prayer mats. Sometimes it's my job to suggest alternative solutions, like having the staff trained to be aware of things like this. So, all-in-all, I have a pretty holistic job as a chaplain.

CORPORATE LEADERSHIP

An important aspect of leadership among Australian Muslims is corporate leadership. This can be seen at three different levels, or tiers:

* Islamic societies of each state and territory;
* Islamic council of each state and territory; and
* the Australian Federation of Islamic Councils (AFIC).

Muslim societies and associations, in theory at least, are networked through the relevant state Islamic council. All state councils are then represented at a national level by the AFIC.

All three tiers are governed by constitutions. Revolving membership of corporate bodies is largely composed of lay leaders, rather than imams who have been specifically trained in the Islamic religious disciplines. This is partly due to the distance that often exists between imams and the local culture and language. Hence, it is the lay leadership which plays a fairly substantial role in representing Muslims to politicians, the government, the media and other non-Muslim community organisations.

Whether a productive relationship exists between these three tiers of corporate organisation of Muslim communities is debatable. Tension among Muslim communities can be reflected in the area of leadership and can involve ethnic, political and religious quarrels among and between the three tiers. Disputes do arise within a society or state council, between one society and another, between a society and a council, or even between a council and AFIC.

In the 1960s, attempts were made to organise Australia's Muslim communities, and a major step in the process was the founding of the Australian Federation of Islamic Societies (AFIS), a national organisation. Established in 1964 by leading Muslims such as Fehmi al-Imam, Abdul Khaliq Kazi and Ibrahim Dellal, AFIS served as an umbrella organisation to coordinate various important Muslim activities. The organisation represented Muslims from different ethnic backgrounds: Indians, Pakistanis, Egyptians, Lebanese and Turks all participated. Eventually the AFIS evolved into the AFIC in 1976. Each state Islamic council representing the various Muslim societies became a member of the AFIC.

Continuing today, among the main areas of interest for the AFIC are the building of mosques and schools, and the certification of halal meat. This latter activity contributed considerable financial strength to the organisation. A substantial quantity of meat is exported to Muslim countries such as Saudi Arabia, Malaysia and Indonesia. Before being exported, the meat must be certified as halal and, given that the certificates are obtained on a fee basis, a substantial income is available from the activity. As well, the AFIC serves as the key Muslim advocacy group with the federal government and has been active in this role since the 1970s. Today, tensions within the Muslim communities and challenges to the AFIC's authority have somewhat weakened its influence. Furthermore, the decentralisation of halal meat certification has taken away the quasi-monopoly the AFIC once enjoyed in this area. Despite this, the AFIC still functions as an umbrella organisation for many Muslims, although it has not been successful in bringing together several independent Muslim societies to create a strong, unified movement to lobby for the interests of all Muslims in Australia.

COLLECTIVE RELIGIOUS LEADERSHIP?

Although there are several leadership positions existing within Muslim communities in Australia, there have not been many significant attempts to bring together nominated religious leaders or one single religious leader to represent the entire population of Australian Muslims, notwithstanding some community desire for such a position. Because of the number of ethnic, political and theological differences that exist among Australian Muslims, it would be extremely difficult for one chosen person to acceptably represent the Muslim community as a whole.

For some, the closest person to such a figure is Taj al-Din al-Hilali, an imam based in Sydney. He is referred to by some Muslims and non-Muslims as the 'Mufti of Australia'. The title of 'Mufti' (a person who is entitled to issue *fatwa*, or religious edicts) was apparently given by the AFIC Congress to Taj al-Din during the campaign waged in the 1980s by certain groups in the Muslim and Lebanese communities to have him deported. The Immigration Minister, Mr Hurford, was determined to deport him and apparently this was a tactic used by the AFIC to try to stay that procedure. Not all Muslims in Australia consider him to be the 'Mufti of Australia', nor do they recognise his fatwas. Like any imam in Australia, he has a strong following in certain sections of the Muslim community, particularly in Lakemba, Sydney.

In the 1990s, however, something close to a collective religious leadership began to emerge with the establishment of a Board of Imams in various states of Australia, such as New South Wales and Victoria. Each Board brings together imams of mosques in order to discuss and make decisions on matters of interest to Muslims. Although a Board theoretically represents imams of all mosques in the state, in practice only a small number actually take part in the weekly or monthly meetings and contribute to the decision-making process. Whether these Boards of Imams will evolve into a collective religious leadership at the national level is not entirely clear. It is a possibility, however, that at present seems unlikely. A national conference of imams was called by the AFIC in 1998 in order to give some national cohesion to the leadership of imams, but this initiative has not been followed up by subsequent conferences.

WHO IS SPEAKING ON BEHALF OF WHOM?

This leads us to the question of who is speaking on behalf of whom? On any religious issue, is there one single authority to which Muslims turn? Although the so-called Mufti of Australia is one such possibility, given doubts over the degree of recognition that he is accorded makes this unlikely.

Another possible source is the Boards of Imams; however, there is no single entity for the whole of Australia and, in practice, each imam generally speaks on behalf of his immediate religious community, or at least some members of that community. Since the September 11 bombings and the subsequent backlash against Muslims in Australia, there have been calls for a unified Muslim voice on religious issues. Whether or not this becomes a reality, it is impossible to prevent many others in the community from expressing their opinions, particularly influential lay leaders.

Given this, it is possible to say that there is no one person or group of people who can speak on behalf of the entire Muslim community, even on religious matters. The community is divided theologically, in religious orientation, in terms of ethnicity and approaches to Islam in Australia. Furthermore, there are Muslims whose commitment to Islam varies from total allegiance to almost total rejection. Thus, a single religious leader could not speak on behalf of such a diverse range of people. Historically, Muslim communities have accepted and manifested diversity within their boundaries, and this is even more the case with Australia. The only conclusion that can be reached is that religious leadership in the Australian Muslim community will remain divided for the foreseeable future.

Chapter 10

HALAL FOOD

Halal means 'permitted under Islamic law'. The term halal can be used in the context of food—such as halal meat or halal food—or it can also be used with things like halal income, meaning income earned by using halal means. In this chapter, we will look at the issue of halal food.

The substantial growth of halal food outlets is another feature of Muslim institutional life in Australia. In connection with food, halal refers to those products that are prepared in accordance with Islamic religious requirements, or to the avoidance of non-permissible food products. Islam teaches that a Muslim should:

- not consume ham, pork and other pig-based products;
- not consume wine and other alcoholic beverages; and
- eat meat (such as beef, lamb, chicken) only if the animals and birds are slaughtered according to certain guidelines.

There is debate among Australian Muslims over whether (non-pig) meat from animals slaughtered in Australian abattoirs can be eaten by Muslims. Generally speaking, there are two main views on this issue.

Following classical Islamic law and prominent Muslim scholars of today, such as Yusuf al-Qaradawi, some Muslims believe that animals slaughtered by Christians and Jews can be eaten by Muslims. As long as the animal is *slaughtered*, its meat is halal and thus can be eaten. For them, buying meat from an Australian supermarket or any butcher is therefore acceptable. Similarly, they would feel comfortable eating meat in a restaurant that does not declare itself as a halal restaurant.

However, many other Muslims are not so lenient on this issue. For them, meat can be consumed only if the animal is slaughtered by a Muslim, and therefore they will go to a halal meat shop to buy their meat. They would not eat at a non-halal restaurant for fear that the restaurant might be serving non-halal meat or using the same utensils for cooking pig-meat, and that it might be using alcohol or animal fat (particularly lard) in the preparation of food.

Those Muslims who are the strictest as far as halal meat is concerned are particularly careful with the ingredients in various food items available in the supermarket. Halal food has become much more than just avoiding pig-meat, meat of animals slaughtered by methods which do not follow Islamic requirements, and alcoholic beverages. It has become also an exercise in identifying ingredients which are considered 'non-halal', not only in food items but also in detergents, soaps, toothpaste and shampoo. They will go to great lengths to avoid any item that contains

certain ingredients. One Muslim website concerned with halal food products advises Muslims as follows:

> Muslims should make a habit of examining the ingredients label on every food and drink package before consuming it. Items which contain one or more *haram* [prohibited] ingredient(s) should be rejected. Only those items which contain all halal ingredients should be chosen for consumption . . . Muslims are advised to get acquainted with the nature of the most commonly used ingredients in the food industry and food additive code numbers.[1]

The site goes on to say that Muslims must avoid food that contains the following ingredients: lard, gelatin, pepsin, rennet, enzymes (except *microbial* enzymes) and whey.

In a document prepared by the Islamic Council of Queensland for health professionals, the following instructions were provided in relation to food to be served at hospitals:[2]

> All kitchen staff should be aware that only halal meat (that is, meat slaughtered according to religious requirements) must be given to Muslim patients. They should also be made aware that Muslims do not eat pork or any other pig meat and its products, eg bacon, ham sausages, etc. Separate utensils should be used for preparing food. For example, the knife used for slicing pork must not be used to cut anything to be given to a Muslim.
>
> Halal food should be made available to Muslim patients. If this is not possible, Muslims should be given the choice of having seafood, eggs, fruit and vegetables.
>
> Pig meat and all its products are forbidden to Muslims,

together with wild animals that use their claws or teeth to kill their victims, all birds of prey, rodents, reptiles, worms and the like, and dead animals and birds that are not slaughtered properly according to Islamic rites. Alcohol and any other intoxicating substances are prohibited in Islam. Muslims are allowed to eat all seafood and dairy products.

This document goes on to list foods approved (halal) and prohibited (non-halal) by the Islamic faith:

Meat and substitutes
Halal: Chicken, beef, lamb killed by Muslim slaughtermen; all seafood; eggs cooked in water, butter, vegetable margarine or vegetable oil; dried beans and lentils, baked beans
Non-halal: Pork and all pig products (e.g. bacon, ham, salami)

Milk and milk products
Halal: Milk, yoghurt, cheese, ice cream made without animal fat, eg tofu ice cream, gelati or sherbet
Non-halal: Ice cream made with animal fat

Fruit and vegetables
Halal: All fruit or vegetables: raw, dried, canned or cooked using water, vegetable fats or butter
Non-halal: Any fried or roasted in lard or dripping

Bread and cereals
Halal: All breakfast cereals. Bread, cakes and biscuits prepared without animal fat other than butter. Rice cooked without animal fat. Pasta

Fats and oils
Halal: Butter, vegetable margarine, olive oil, peanut oil, vegetable oils
Non-halal: Lard, dripping, suet, other animal fats (except butter) and any other foods made with or cooked in them

Beverages
Halal: Tea, coffee, water, fruit juices, soft drinks, mineral and soda water, cordials
Non-halal: Alcohol and foods cooked with alcohol, eg trifles, puddings, sauces

Soups
Halal: Any made without pork, ham or animal fats
Non-halal: Any with ham or bone stock

Desserts
Halal: Any without alcohol, lard, dripping or suet, eg fruit-based, custards, tofu ice cream, gelati or sherbet, puddings made with butter or vegetable margarine, egg dishes, rice dishes
Non-halal: Any with alcohol, lard, suet, dripping, ice cream with animal fat

Miscellaneous
Halal: Coconut milk, spices including chilli, curry powder, pickles, chutneys
Non-halal: Gelatine (pork product), vanilla essence (alcohol based)

When Muslims began establishing themselves in Australia, some of the first businesses to be operated were halal butchers and meat shops. Today, in all major cities of Australia, there is a plethora of halal food outlets, restaurants and even some supermarkets providing halal meat and other products to their Muslim customers. In shopping centres in Melbourne and Sydney, especially in suburbs which have a significant Muslim population, it is not difficult to find food outlets with the label 'halal'. Turkish, Lebanese, Indian and Malay restaurants and takeaways are abundant in areas such as Brunswick, Coburg and Campbellfield in Melbourne and in suburbs such as Auburn in Sydney. Muslims and non-Muslims may eat at these outlets, as 'halal' does not mean much more than avoidance of certain food items. The Internet plays a major role in familiarising Muslims with the locations of halal butchers, meat shops and restaurants.

The halal food market is huge in global terms. Given that approximately one-fifth of the world's population is Muslim, the demand for halal foods—from meat and dairy products to chocolate and biscuits—is strong. Australia is a key player in exporting halal food, most notably meat and dairy products, to this ever-expanding market. In this, Australian Muslims are playing an increasingly important role in developing export markets.

Chapter 11

ISLAMIC SCHOOLS

In the 1950s, Muslim parents and volunteers began to establish Islamic 'weekend schools' in Melbourne and Sydney, but there were scant resources and few people had enough knowledge to thoroughly instruct the children on Islam. Despite the difficulties, parents would send their children for a few hours on either Saturday or Sunday to a local mosque or a prayer facility in order to gain a religious education.

Children still attend these weekend schools, where they are taught how to read the Qur'an (in Arabic) and gain a basic knowledge of the religion and of what they are expected to do as Muslims. In many cases, the language of the parents (be it Arabic, Turkish, Urdu or any other) is also taught. The parents feel responsible for providing at least a basic knowledge of Islam, as well as of their home culture and language. Today, these weekend classes are held at mosques, prayer facilities, local Islamic centres and even at rented public school facilities. Teachers are often volunteers who may not have a formal teaching qualification. Each local community organises its weekend school, and there is no umbrella organisation for these schools or a common curriculum.

As well as weekend schools, Muslims have established a number of regular schools providing primary and secondary education, along with instruction in Arabic and Islam. Islamic schools in Australia are part of the faith-based school system, such as that of Catholic, Lutheran, Greek Orthodox, Coptic Christian and Jewish schools. The first such school—the King Khalid Islamic College (KKIC)—was established in 1983 in the northern suburbs of Melbourne with funding received from overseas as well as local sources. Since then, other Islamic schools have been established in Victoria, and New South Wales, Western Australia, Queensland and South Australia. Many of these schools offer both primary- and secondary-level education, while some focus on the primary level only. Student numbers vary greatly: the more established schools, such as the KKIC in Victoria and the Malek Fahd Islamic School in Sydney, each have well over 1000 students; those newly established mostly have around 300–500 students. These schools rely very heavily on government funding. In most cases, around 80 per cent of the funding for the running of the school comes from the government. The fees charged also vary from as low as $600 to $2000 per annum. However, many Muslim parents do not send their children to Islamic schools for a variety of reasons, ranging from inability to pay the fees or concerns with the standard of the school, to the absence of an Islamic school in their area or simply lack of interest. Given that the number of students in Islamic schools is around 12 000 to 15 000, one could say that Islamic schools are serving a relatively small percentage of the Muslim children in Australia. Most Muslim children go to the state schools. Some Muslim parents send their children to Catholic schools, as these schools often provide a single-sex environment and a moral education in their curriculum, while the state schools are co-educational and ignore religious education. Middle- to upper-middle-class Muslims often send their children to well-regarded private schools.

Islamic schools have also become the target of much criticism in the media. Some commentators see Islamic schools as divisive, preventing full participation of their female students in education and Australian society. Others see the values underpinning Islamic schools as in conflict with traditional Australian values. In response to such accusations, Islamic schools argue that such criticisms are unfair and unwarranted. They argue that their curricula are those of the state educational authorities and their activities are monitored by these very authorities.

Broadly speaking, some of the stated aims of the Islamic schools are as follows:

- To achieve the highest possible standard of moral behaviour and ethical attitudes.
- To provide the children with an Islamic environment free from undesirable social values.
- To develop and foster a complete Muslim identity and personality within the child.

- To equip the children with the necessary knowledge, skills, attitudes and behaviours to enable them to contribute meaningfully to the general harmony, prosperity and good of their community and the overall society.

King Khalid Islamic College:
The first Islamic school in Australia

Established in 1983, King Khalid Islamic College has two campuses in the northern suburbs of Melbourne, close to the heavily Muslim-populated areas of Brunswick, Coburg, Fawkner and Broadmeadows. The Coburg campus provides primary-level education, while its Merlynston campus is a co-educational Islamic school providing secondary level education (Year 7 to 12). At the college, boys and girls study together and there is, generally speaking, no segregation. Girls wear a headscarf which covers their hair and neck. The college population has a wide variety of teachers and students from different ethnic backgrounds, including European, Arab, East African, Indian, Pakistani, Malay, Indonesian, South African and Turkish. The vast majority of its students are born in Australia. The college states that it recognises that Australia is a nation of immigrants and cherishes the multi-racial, multicultural and multi-faith nature and aspirations of our society and encourages all its students to cultivate a world wide outlook on life and to constantly seek to broaden their horizons with regard to tolerance, compassion and co-operation with one another.

The College curriculum is balanced between secular and Islamic education. Students are being taught to be proud of their Islamic identity and of being Australian Muslims. Apart from the Holy Qur'an and LOTE (languages other than English), all subjects are taught in English. Arabic language and Religious Studies are taught at all levels.

Other early Islamic schools include Al-Noori Muslim Primary School (1983) and Malek Fahd Islamic School (1989), both in Sydney, as well as Australian Islamic College (1986) in Perth. At the time of writing, there are 25 Islamic schools in all major Australian cities, but the majority are based in Sydney and Melbourne.

The performance of these schools varies greatly. Those that were established earliest, such as KKIC, appear to be performing well. In fact, KKIC is among the few select schools in Victoria that offer the International Baccalaureate (IB) program in addition to the Victorian Certificate of Education (VCE). Several Islamic schools, including KKIC and the Perth-based Australian Islamic College, have produced students who were among the top achievers in their final year of schooling in that state. However, many new Islamic schools are still attempting to establish themselves. Many are located in lower socio-economic 'disadvantaged' areas and, given the short history of these schools, it will take some time before they become as established as KKIC.

Although funding for *starting* many Islamic schools initially came mostly from overseas, their continuing existence has depended on Australian government funding. Schools based in disadvantaged areas, such as the northern suburbs of Melbourne and working-class areas in Sydney, attract generous subsidies from the government. As such, they can often provide *relatively* comparable education to other schools functioning in the state. These Islamic schools teach the local state curriculum, supervised by the state Department of Education.

One of the difficulties for both weekend and regular Islamic schools is the lack of Islamic religious education teaching materials, such as textbooks that are appropriate to an Australian context. Many schools use material developed in Europe, the United States, Turkey, Lebanon, Syria or Saudi Arabia, and adapted as much as possible to Australian needs and context. The twin challenges of finding qualified teaching staff and appropriate curricula for Islamic religious education are a problem not only for Muslims in Australia, but also for even older Muslim-minority communities in the West.

According to the International Board of Educational Research and Resources, which is interested in developing suitable curriculum materials for Islamic studies, some of the shortcomings of the Islamic studies teaching materials generally available are a lack of colour and design, unsuitable grading, out of reach of the psychological world of children, and lack of activities and effective exercises.

One might add to this list the lack of Australian content in these curriculum materials.

Islamic schools employ teachers from different ethnic and religious backgrounds. Many teachers in Islamic schools are, in fact, non-Muslim. It is only in the area of Islamic religious instruction that teachers are usually required to be Muslim, as parents prefer that their children are taught the religion by fellow Muslims. In all other areas, the teaching staff and curriculum are much like any other public school.

Among the main differences between Islamic schools and public schools are the three or four hours per week devoted to Islamic religious education, as well as the observance of certain Islamic norms such as the holding of noon (Zuhr) prayers, celebration of some Islamic occasions, provision of halal food in the school canteen and the existence of an Islamic dress code. Generally speaking, the girls' uniforms include long-sleeved shirts or blouses, skirts, pants or long socks covering the legs and below the knees. They also usually include headscarves. Boys wear shirts and long pants, as shorts above the knee are not considered acceptable. All in all, students experience school life within the context of Islamic norms of practice appropriate to Australian life. One of the key objectives of these schools is to provide education for children to enable them to function effectively in Australian life while remaining faithful to their religion, Islam.

Islamic schools

New South Wales

Al-Noori Muslim Primary School, Greenacre (1983)
Arkana College, Beverly Hills (1986)
Malek Fahd Islamic School, Greenacre (1989)
Noor Al Houda Islamic College (Girls), Condell Park (1995)

Sule College, Prestons (1996)
Al-Amanah College, Bankstown (1997)
King Abdul Aziz College, Rooty Hill (1997)
Risalah Islamic College Ltd, Lakemba (1997)
Al-Zahra College, Arncliffe (1998)
Al-Faisal College, Auburn (1998)

Victoria

King Khalid Islamic College of Victoria, Coburg (1983)
Islamic Schools of Victoria (Werribee College), Hoppers
    Crossing (1986)
Minaret College, Springvale (1993)
Islamic College, Broadmeadows (1995)
Darul Uloom Islamic College, Fawkner (1997)
Isik College, Broadmeadows (1997)
East Preston Islamic College, Preston (1998)

Western Australia

Australian Islamic College, Dianella (1986)
Australian Islamic College, Thornlie (1990)
Al Hidayah Islamic School Inc, Bentley (1994)
Australian Islamic College, Kewdale (2000)

Queensland

Islamic School of Brisbane Ltd, Karawatha (1995)

South Australia

Islamic College, Croydon (1998)

Chapter 12

MUSLIM WOMEN

A view that is widely held among Australians is that women in Muslim societies, and even in Australian Muslim communities, are often subject to discrimination, oppression and injustice. It is believed that in many Muslim communities women are treated as second-class citizens or, worse, as less than human beings. This is largely based on the following:

- In some Muslim societies, a man may have up to four wives simultaneously, but a woman may have only one husband at any given time.
- Many Muslim women wear a veil or headscarf and this is seen as a symbol of oppression, forced upon women by the dictates of the Islamic religion.
- In a few Muslim communities, girls are discouraged from going to school beyond primary level; women are not allowed to drive; they do not have the right to vote or take part in

the political sphere; and they are not allowed to work outside the home except in very limited arenas.

- Images of women in Afghanistan (widely shown on television screens around the world, particularly in the post-September 11 period) showed the awful state of women under the Taliban who claimed that their views on women were sanctioned by Islam.

- Islamic law is viewed as discriminatory against women in a number of areas. Commonly cited is the case of inheritance laws, where in certain situations a woman is allotted half the share of a man. For instance, if a parent leaves an estate to be distributed, a son will receive double the share of the daughter.

A glance at the thousands of Muslim communities around the world—including those in Australia—would reveal that there is a substantial degree of diversity in how Muslim communities treat their men and women. In some Muslim communities, men and women are considered equal and there are laws to protect this equality. However, in several Muslim communities, there is systematic discrimination against women. This can be in a number of areas, such as employment, political participation and education. Women in these societies are largely confined to taking care of the household.

Much of this diversity in practice is the result of local cultural practices, values and norms. There is a substantial difference in how women are treated in Afghanistan (particularly under the Taliban) and, for example, Tunisia, Indonesia, Iran, Egypt and Malaysia. Although the situation differs somewhat from country to country, and even within one country from region to region or from class to class, women in all these latter countries generally enjoy rights equal to men in many areas. Iran, for instance, considered by many in the West as one of the most conservative Muslim societies, has women professors, parliamentarians, bureaucrats and ministers at all levels of society. Women's representation in all levels of government in Iran is comparable to that of some Western countries. This representation allows women to participate in formulating policies that affect not only women, but also the whole society. On another note, in Muslim-majority countries such as Turkey, Pakistan, Bangladesh and Indonesia, women have held the positions of prime minister or president. Despite this one cannot deny the existence of varying degrees of restrictions on women even in the most enlightened Muslim societies.

DEBATE ON THE ROLE OF WOMEN IN SOCIETY

Among Australian Muslim women, the debate on the role of women in society is an ongoing and vigorous one. There appear to be three main trends in this debate: Traditionalist, Liberal and neo-Modernist. The Traditionalist view appears to be held by a relatively small but vocal number of Australian Muslim women. The vast majority of women appear to subscribe to the neo-Modernist or Liberal view.

The Traditionalist view

There is a small but vocal group of Australian Muslim women who argue that the role of women should be as it is envisaged in classical Islamic law. For them, women's role should be more narrowly restricted to the home and their primary task is looking after their children and husband. They argue for maintaining segregation, and wear the hijab to cover their hair and neck, and at times their face as well. They avoid places where men and women mix, and believe that women who argue for a view other than the Traditionalist position are not sufficiently religious. They are highly critical of Muslim women who do not wear the hijab.

This view is also adopted by some converts to Islam from European backgrounds.

The Liberal view

There are Australian Muslim women who reject this Traditionalist view as antiquarian and irrelevant. For them, much of the Muslims' discourse of the past on women has become irrelevant for Muslim women of today. Compromises and inter-pretations to adapt classical Islamic texts to contemporary problems related to women's issues are not needed. What is needed, they believe, is a fresh look to be taken at the position of women in Muslim societies, the fight for full equality and the rejection of all symbols of patriarchal domination of women. For them, the hijab is a symbol of oppression and an unneces-sary relic from the past and should be rejected. Islam, for them, is not in need of such superficial symbols. They may or may not be practising Muslims. As one practising woman put it, 'I pray five times a day but at home. I don't go to the mosque because of the separation between men and women in prayer, which for me is a sign of domination of women by men. I hate that.'

The neo-Modernist view

A position that is popular among many Australian women is that there is no inherent conflict between Islam (as evidenced in the Qur'an and traditions of the Prophet) and the needs and aspirations of Muslim women today. They argue that men and women should be equal and that the role of women in Muslim societies historically has been misinterpreted. Among those who advocate this position are young Muslim women who grew up in Australia, many Muslim converts and other Muslim women of a more liberal mind. These women believe in the essential equality of men and women in the eyes of God and in society. They assert the independence of women, consider important the playing of an active role in society by women, and argue for equal opportunities in all areas of education, political participation and decision making in society. They reject the idea that women cannot take responsibility for themselves and that a man should always be there to support them. They rely on the Qur'an and sunna to support their position and reject interpretations that go against their position. Given the apparent popularity of this view, particularly among those who are 'committed to Islam'—that is, practising Muslim women—the rest of this chapter attempts to present in some detail the position of the neo-Modernists on a number of questions relating to the role of Muslim women in Australia.

WHAT DOES ISLAM SAY ABOUT WOMEN?

Muslim women of a neo-Modernist persuasion believe that, in order to understand what Islam says about women, we need to go back to the Qur'an and the traditions of the Prophet, not to the interpretations of the following generations. They believe that fourteen centuries ago, in the patriarchal Arabian society, the Qur'an and the Prophet Muhammad gave women many rights that have been ignored in the subsequent development of Islam. For them, the true nature of Islamic teachings is found in the Qur'an and the traditions of the Prophet. In both, there is much material to support women's arguments for equality and equal rights in society today. Some of the examples are as follows:

- Men and women are equal in the eyes of God. According to the Qur'an:

  > God has got ready forgiveness and tremendous rewards for Muslim men and women; the believing men and women; the devout men and women; the truthful men and women; the patiently suffering men and women; the humble men and women; the almsgiving men and women; the fasting men and women; the men and women who guard their chastity; and the men and women who are exceedingly mindful of God (33:35).

- Men and women are complementary to each other. The Qur'an says:

  > The believers, men and women, are protectors of one another: they enjoin what is just, and forbid what is evil:

they observe regular prayers, practise regular charity, and obey God and His Messenger (9:71–72).

- A woman is an independent person. Even in marriage, she maintains her independence. For example, a Muslim woman retains her own name after marriage. Similarly, a woman cannot be forced into marriage even by her father. She has the right of refusal. During the time of the Prophet, a woman by the name of Khansa was given in marriage by her father, without her permission. After complaining to the Prophet, he gave her the option of annulling the marriage.

- A woman has the right to own property and to retain that right after marriage. Her husband has no right to her property or wealth—in fact, he should provide for her and the children even if she is wealthy. Her property remains her own and she can do whatever she wants with it.

- A woman has the right to include terms and clauses which protect her in the marriage contract. The Prophet's own great-grand-daughter, Sukayna, reportedly sued one husband in court for violating the contractual provision of monogamy and maintained the right of autonomy in all her marriage contracts.

For these women, the Qur'an taught the idea of the creation of men and women as equal, rather than viewing woman as a 'type' or 'by-product' of man. Moreover, in the story of Adam and Eve, rather than viewing the latter as responsible for the fall of man, in the version in the Qur'an Satan tempted both of the original parents who, after realising their mistake, repented and were forgiven. Unlike views prevailing in some other religious traditions, there is no debate among Muslims over whether a woman possesses a soul or whether she will go to heaven. From an Islamic perspective, such views have no legitimate religious basis, since men and women are equal before God and complementary to each other. The differences that do exist are simply of biological necessity rather than signalling a disparity in the value or worth of a person.

For neo-Modernists, these positive attitudes and ideas about women, expressed in the Qur'an and by the Prophet, were revolutionary in the seventh century. But many of the ideas that Islam introduced in this domain were swept away or modified in the following centuries under the weight of local cultural norms, values and practices. The liberationary discourse of the Qur'an about women and their rights was sidelined in a number of cultures. What we find in 21st-century Muslim communities around the world is often a hotch-potch of local cultural practices juxtaposed with some Islamic ideas, but often all simply labelled as 'Islamic'.

For example, these women believe that the Taliban in Afghanistan attempted to justify their mistreatment of women by claiming to implement Islam, but their brand of the religion was almost unrecognisable to the vast majority of the world's Muslims. In most of the 56 Muslim-majority countries, the Taliban's treatment of women in the name of Islam would simply not have been tolerated. In a very few countries, women are required to wear the veil and are prohibited from driving a car or voting. Again, these practices are justified by reference to Islam; however, most Muslim countries do not recognise these as Islamic practices, and justify their own interpretation of equal rights also using Islamic terms and texts. Thus, we can see that the appeal to religion can throw up a wide diversity of practices ranging from Taliban oppression on the one hand, to women being voted into the highest office of the land, on the other. It is impossible to talk about the experience of Muslim women as being uniformly positive or negative.

Monogamy and Polygyny

An extremely controversial area is that of polygyny (also called polygamy), which permits a Muslim man to take up to four wives. Although this permission was given in the seventh century based on a certain socio-historical context and with strict conditions, polygyny has continued to be practised in the modern period. It is a sensitive area, as for many, polygyny is seen as degrading to women, as maintaining inequality and as a step backwards into the pre-modern era. Because of this, the practice has been on the receiving end of substantial challenges from both within and without the Muslim world.

Today, a number of Muslim countries have severely restricted the practice of polygyny. More importantly, the vast majority of Muslims in the world are monogamous. Polygyny is practised in some societies; however, in others, it is either forbidden or severely restricted, and a man has to apply to a court for permission to take a second wife. Marriage contracts are also used by women and men to specify monogamy, and in some Muslim cultures polygyny is unthinkable. As with many other facets of Muslim life, the practice varies widely depending on context, culture, social attitudes and other factors. In Australia, despite polygyny being illegal, the debate continues among Muslims.

Traditionalists among Australian Muslims argue that as polygyny was permitted in Islam in the beginnning, it cannot be prohibited just because of changes in attitudes and values. Traditionalists, as well as those who come from cultures in which the institution is widely practised, usually take this position. Interestingly, even among Traditionalist women, often one comes across arguments against polygyny but more on personal grounds than religious ones. Even if polygyny were legally valid in Australia, the vast majority of Muslim women probably would not choose to be members of polygynous households, reflecting worldwide practice. The prevailing ideas in Australia on monogamy dominate the thinking on this issue among Muslims, particularly second- and third-generation Muslims.

Neo-Modernists argue that Islam was not the first religion to permit or condone polygyny; in fact, it was practised by many different cultures and communities, including biblical ones. As far as its practice today is concerned, for many in the neo-Modernist camp, there is no general *endorsement* of polygyny in Islam and the permission accorded by the Qur'an only applied to certain circumstances and conditions. They feel that a careful reading of the texts in the Qur'an relating to the issue of polygyny demonstrates that the qur'anic intention appears to be to abolish the practice, but that would have been impossible in the seventh century.

Those who argue against polygyny today take the line that, before Islam, men could and did take an unrestricted number of wives, who were treated virtually as sexual chattels. Islam, in fact, placed severe restrictions on the practice and made it conditional upon justice and equal treatment. Therefore, as the Qur'an restricted polygyny even in the seventh century, there is no reason, they believe, why Muslims should not restrict the practice completely today, based on the idea that the conditions which allowed its permission in the seventh century no longer exist in the 21st, particularly in societies like Australia. Interestingly, as there are more Muslim men than women in Australia, neo-Modernists argue that polygyny cannot be supported even on a demographic basis.

Australian law does not allow the marriage of a man to more than one woman at a time. However, given that there is no legal restriction on men and women having multiple partners at the same time (although not officially recognised through marriage), those wishing to practise de-facto polygyny would have little difficulty in so doing. Neo-Modernists argue that this would be unacceptable, given that the institution of marriage is supposed to be a legally and contractually binding public display of commitment. In protecting the rights of the marriage partners, a second, third or fourth wife must have the same legal rights as the first. In Australia it would be almost impossible to guarantee equal legal rights to all marriage partners, given the laws in place.

Contact between men and women

Another controversial issue is that of segregation of women and men. In a small number of Muslim communities, women are kept secluded from the rest of the community. For example, in

Saudi Arabia, and more recently Afghanistan, total segregation is observed and women are required to cover their entire bodies—including their faces—so that they cannot be recognised. In other countries where there is more latitude, such as Pakistan, women are still largely segregated and kept separate in many social arenas. Although the majority of Muslim countries do not practise segregation or consider women to be second-class citizens, the apparent religious sanction that these practices obtain in some quarters has linked Islam with a lack of female autonomy and emancipation.

While Traditionalists are comfortable with and accept the idea of segregation, neo-Modernists argue that segregation is not necessarily 'Islamic'. Relying on the events of early Islamic history, they argue that women should play an equally important role in society as men. For them, in the Prophet's own time, women played key roles in the establishment of the new religion. Khadija, his first wife, who proposed marriage to the young Muhammad after employing him in her business, was the first convert to Islam. She provided financial and emotional support to the Prophet and he remained devoted to her until the end of her life. Muslim women fought alongside men in battles, as well as providing nursing aid and offering moral support. Early Muslim women also played key administrative roles: Ayesha, the Prophet's wife, was a scholar and led an army in battle. A woman, Shaffa, was appointed by the caliph Umar as a supervisor of the market (a position equivalent to a senior bureaucrat). According to neo-Modernists, the picture of Muslim women as shy, retiring creatures hidden away at home certainly does not figure in such strong role models.

Today, in Australia, women play an active part in the affairs of Muslim communities. Muslim women study and teach in both Muslim and non-Muslim schools and universities. Groups such as the Islamic Women's Welfare Council of Victoria perform social work and care for new migrants. The Muslim Women's National Network of Australia, among other things, represents the interests of Muslim women at the state and federal levels and provides education to Muslim and non-Muslim groups on social issues. Women are also represented in various levels of Muslim administrative bodies, as well as generally being active in supporting the Muslim communities of Australia. However, women often still face Traditionalists' attempts to marginalise them in areas where women have to work with men.

Arranged marriages

Neo-Modernists argue there is nothing in the Qur'an or the traditions of the Prophet to suggest that arranged marriages are promoted by Islam. Rather, the arranging of marriages is a cultural practice that exists in both Muslim and non-Muslim societies. In India, for instance, such marriages are common among Muslims, Hindus, Sikhs, Christians and Buddhists. The practice exists in other parts of Asia and Africa, and is not specifically an Islamic institution. In many parts of the Muslim world, arranged marriages are not common, while in others they are. What is specified in Islam is that marriage is a contract entered into willingly by two parties. A woman cannot be forced to accept a marriage if she does not want it. She has the right to refuse such a marriage.

Islamic dress code

Women's dress is often viewed as an obstacle to female emancipation, and as proof of misogyny and inequality.

Neo-Modernists argue that, contrary to popular belief, Islam
promotes a dress code in the form of general guidelines for *both*
men and women. These general guidelines are then interpreted
in a plethora of different ways by Muslims who live in a variety
of different contexts, cultures and societies. Generally speaking,
Islam promotes the concepts of modesty and chastity, and
emphasises the non-exploitation of male and female bodies by
desexualising them in the public sphere and de-emphasising class-
or wealth-based displays of status. If women cover up more than
men, it is simply a reflection of the biological differences between
men and women, and is not an indication of worth. Many
Muslim women argue that conforming to the Islamic dress code
is a way of saying that they wish to be valued by factors other
than the size, shape or appearance of their body.

Guidelines for men

At a minimum, the man's body between the navel and the knee
should be covered. He should wear loose, rather than form-
fitting, clothes made of a cloth that is opaque rather than
transparent. He should avoid clothes made of pure silk and
should not wear gold jewellery.

There is no one standard 'Islamic dress' for men. In different
parts of the Muslim world, different types of clothes are worn.
They may range from a gown-like garment with a head cover
for Arabs in the Gulf; to a shirt and sarong in India; to *shalwar*

and *qamis* in Pakistan; to loose jeans and a shirt in Australia. In a number of Muslim cultures men also cover their hair using a variety of covering garments. Tuareg men in Africa even cover their faces. In Australia, it is easy to find Muslims wearing a variety of clothes which represent Muslim cultures from around the world on a Friday at the mosque or during the Eid prayers and celebrations.

GUIDELINES FOR WOMEN

It is usually understood that the minimum to be covered is the whole body except for the face, hands and feet. The clothes should be loose rather than form-fitting, and opaque rather than transparent. Unlike men, women may wear gold and other forms of jewellery and silk clothes.

Again, there is no one standard 'Islamic dress' for women, and different types of clothes are worn in different parts of the Muslim world. Some women wear blouses and skirts; others wear shirts and pants; still others wear a gown-like garment; Pakistanis often wear shalwar and qamis; others wear shirts and jeans. Some women cover their faces and wear black; others wear scarves of different colours and patterns. Some women wear the latest designer clothes from Paris and New York, while others wear traditional clothes of the local culture.

The majority of Muslim women believe that covering the face is not a requirement, and there are some disputes among Muslims on whether a woman should cover her hair. Some Muslim women believe that covering the hair is not really a religious requirement but a cultural one. They argue that as a Muslim woman does not have to cover her hair, there is no need for a head cover. Others disagree and argue that this is indeed a religious requirement. Still others feel that wearing a headscarf is a way of demonstrating their Islamic identity. Many Muslim women around the world do not cover their hair, while plenty of others do and follow other aspects of the dress code. There is a common misconception that women are forced to wear the headscarf against their will. In fact, wearing the scarf is often a source of pride for many Muslim women, and the family and friends of a Muslim woman may congratulate her and celebrate the adoption of the scarf if she has recently begun to wear it. In Australia, Muslim women wearing scarves are seen in major cities and towns, on university campuses, in schools and factories, and at counters in shopping centres. Some Australian women cover their entire body (including the face, hands and feet), although this is not generally practised in most parts of the Muslim world.

The 'value' of women

In some Muslim communities, it is believed that a woman is not fully equal to a man. This is based on an interpretation of a qur'anic text in which, instead of a man's testimony, the testimony of a woman is supported by another woman in certain business transactions. Another example given to support the idea that a woman is equivalent to half of a man is that in certain cases of inheritance, a daughter receives half the share of what a son receives.

From the perspective of the neo-Modernists, in the case of a woman's testimony, it is only a precautionary measure where the woman is less familiar with such business practices (as was the case in seventh-century Arabia), rather than being a blanket rule concerning women giving evidence generally. As for the share in inheritance, they argue that this is based on the idea that, under Islamic family law, it is the man's responsibility to provide for the family, including the parents, and the woman has no such financial obligation. For them, this ruling has nothing to do with the relative value of women and men, but rather with equitable provision for those who are required to support others.

Domestic violence

Some people believe that Islam gives a man free rein to discipline his wife, even using physical measures if he so chooses. This is based on an interpretation of a verse of the Qur'an which, as a final resort, allows for the physical disciplining of a woman who has deliberately and persistently acted with ill will and cruelty towards her husband.

According to the neo-Modernists, the interpretation of the verse is a controversial one, as the Prophet himself forbade the beating of any woman ('Never beat God's handmaidens') and many of the greatest mediaeval scholars were of the opinion that physical disciplining should be a symbolic measure only.

Both Traditionalist and neo-Modernist women take the view that domestic violence has no place in Islam. Despite this, like in the Australian community generally, domestic violence is a problem in some sections of the Muslim community. Several Muslim women's organisations exist to help victims of domestic violence among Muslims.

Women and divorce

A perception exists that Muslim women may not initiate divorce and that they have limited rights of release from the marriage contract. In fact, from the neo-Modernists' perspective, a woman may stipulate the right of unilateral divorce in her marriage contract. Apart from this, there are four types of divorce recognised in Islamic law:

- divorce pronounced by the husband;
- divorce by mutual consent (but pronounced by the husband);
- divorce initiated by the wife in which all or part of her dowry (whatever is agreed upon) is returned to the husband; and
- divorce by the court if the wife complains and proves that her husband is neglecting his legal obligations, or is mistreating her in some way.

Given that Australian divorce laws appear to be more favourable to women than Islamic law, and given that divorce in Australia should follow Australian law, the restrictions on women under Islamic law become irrelevant for Australian Muslim women.

Women and mosques

There is a widely held belief in Australia that women should not go to a mosque to perform their prayers or to enjoy fellowship with other Muslims. When television programs or news bulletins feature Muslims praying together, they often show only men, giving the perception that women do not pray or that they do not pray together or in the mosques.

From the neo-Modernists' perspective, early in Muslim history, women used to attend all the prayers. They were specifically encouraged to attend during the major Eid celebrations and to come for lectures and social integration. The Prophet himself said 'Do not stop God's handmaidens from going to God's mosques'. If women felt unable (for one reason or another) to go to a mosque to pray, he encouraged them to pray at home, thus giving them the choice. In time, however, some cultures began to place restrictions on women's movement, and even today there are some mosques whose management may use subtle pressure to dissuade women from attending. Nevertheless, it should be noted that this is contrary to the practice of the Prophet, and is a cultural feature of a few Muslim communities. Neo-Modernists as well as some Traditionalists argue that women may pray in mosques whenever they so choose.

A related issue is that of women praying behind men. Sometimes it is assumed that the status of women is inferior, based on the idea that women pray behind men. Neo-Modernists argue that in fact, the emphasis is merely on forming separate rows during the prayer, particularly as the obligatory salat involves bending and prostrating as well as standing shoulder to shoulder when in congregation. To enable full concentration, men and women pray separately, but this does not give men or women an inferior or superior status. In some mosques—such as in Broadmeadows and Lysterfield in Melbourne—women pray on a level situated above the men. In the Melbourne suburb of Doncaster, the mosque is a long narrow building, and women and men pray in two halves separated by a curtain. So, mosque design does play a part in the spaces given to men and women, as well as the spaces shared by both.

Women's education

The popular view is that Muslim women are oppressed, that they are confined to their homes to look after the family and have no role in society, and that they do not receive a decent education or find work in areas traditionally dominated by males. The reality for Australian Muslim women, however, is very different.

A higher percentage of Muslim women have post-school qualifications in the areas of business and administration, health, education, society and culture, than do Muslim men. Even in other areas which, in the broader Australian society, are dominated by males, Muslim women's participation is significant: they are represented in the natural and physical sciences, as well as engineering, architecture and building, agriculture and related fields (see table below).

Table showing areas of study of Australian Muslims

Fields of study: Muslims (Males and Females)

	Males (%)	Females (%)
Business and administration	48	52
Health	44	56
Education	39	61
Society and culture	47	53
Natural and physical sciences	64	36
Engineering	89	11
Architecture and building	90	10
Agriculture and related fields	81	19

Source: Australian Bureau of Statistics, 1996 Census

The perceived gender inequity among Australian Muslims in the area of education, then, as well as the perceived lack of opportunity for Muslim women to study in traditionally male-dominated areas, is not supported by the statistics. In fact, the Census data show that, compared to the overall Australian population, Muslim women are much more likely than non-Muslim women to participate in historically male-dominated fields such as engineering and architecture. They also show that the gap between Muslim males and females in almost all areas of study is narrower than for the overall Australian population, indicating that the opportunities available for Muslim males and females to pursue higher education are perhaps more gender-balanced than for the overall Australian population.

Ihsanira: Being a Muslim woman

'Seek knowledge even unto China' was a saying of the Prophet Muhammad that has encouraged Muslim men and women for centuries to travel in order to learn and gain education. Because of this I decided to temporarily leave my family in Indonesia (my husband and small children) so that I could come to Australia to study for a Master's degree. Happily, my family also ended up coming to Australia, although it took my husband six months to think about and make the difficult decision; particularly because it has meant that he has changed his role and has taken up a large share of the household tasks while I study. Now I am really happy, because here in Australia I can study on weekdays and have a barbecue with my family on the weekend, and enjoy my spare time by going to the cinema or having a cuppa with my friends.

Another popular view is that Muslim parents do not want their daughters to go beyond a certain basic level of education, and that therefore it is likely that Muslim girls will leave school earlier than non-Muslim girls. In fact, more non-Muslim fifteen- and sixteen-year-old girls are leaving school earlier, and the percentage of girls who are leaving school is higher, than is the case among the Australian Muslim female population.

Muslim girls are also staying at school longer than Muslim boys, which means that Muslim girls have much better educational opportunities in the future than boys. In the overall Australian population, the situation is the reverse: boys are staying on at school and the girls are leaving (1996 Census).

Hena: Being a professional Muslim woman

How does a Muslim react when a punk enters the mosque? Do they welcome them with open arms, or do they hesitate even to speak to them? While Islam teaches us to respect one another, it is only human nature for us to stereotype or form misconceptions about others.

In the same way, when a young Muslim woman like me goes to a country town for work, people not only have to overcome their initial reluctance to speak to a female engineer, but also to one wearing a headscarf. The trick is not to let people's preconceived ideas become a hindrance. Although it is sometimes that extra bit harder to 'prove' myself, once I've broken the ice, there are usually no barriers. I can portray myself as a confident, intelligent Australian engineer. Religion doesn't interfere with my doing all the things I have to do in my job, like escaping from a helicopter simulator turned upside down under water, fire fighting, jumping off a 20-metre platform or travelling to an offshore rig in the middle of the ocean by helicopter. I have not been deprived of any of these activities, and while I set aside some time at work for praying, and consume only restricted foods and drinks, my religion certainly has not hindered me in my professional career.

AUSTRALIAN MUSLIM WOMEN'S STRUGGLE FOR EQUAL RIGHTS

Despite the above somewhat positive picture for Muslim women in Australia (as far as educational opportunities, in particular, are concerned), as elsewhere in the world, much needs to be done to address the issue of equal rights among certain sections of Australian Muslim women. Many Muslim women are going back to the Qur'an and the traditions of the Prophet Muhammad to find out exactly what Islam says about women and women's rights. They are finding that these two sources provide a strong foundation for freeing women from local cultural norms that attempt to limit women's freedom and equality. They do not necessarily view Western models of emancipation as sole solutions or methods for achieving their rights. Some Muslim women rebel against both religious and cultural norms, and follow Western models and ideas of equality. Other Muslim women argue that any type of feminist emphasis is alien to Islam and therefore should be avoided; they follow their local cultural practices, which they see as being Islamic. As with other facets of Muslim life, how women view religion is not uniform: some experience religion as liberating and uplifting; others experience it as enforcing male patriarchy; yet others simply view it as part and parcel of their culture and society.

Several organisations have been founded in each Australian state to improve the lot of Muslim women. Many of these organisations tend to be multi-ethnic, such as the Muslim Women's Association (Lakemba, Sydney), which runs a women's refuge and manages a foster care program; the Islamic Women's Welfare Council of Victoria (Melbourne), which was established in 1991 by a group of interested and concerned women who recognised the need for specialised community services and programs for Muslim women provided by Muslim women; the Islamic Social Services Australia (Melbourne), which runs a foster care program for children; the Islamic Women's Association of Queensland Inc. (Brisbane), which runs an aged-care program and supports Muslim women and children in need; and the Islamic Women's Support Centre (Perth) and Muslim Women's Association of South Australia (Adelaide). All these bodies organise talks, seminars, liaise with government agencies, run anti-discrimination programs and educational sessions, and support women and children in need.

One of the most influential and active Muslim women's groups is the Muslim Women's National Network of Australia Inc., based in Sydney. Its membership is estimated at around 2000 women and it brings together organisations representing Muslim women in all states and territories. The Network has strong links to Muslim organisations in the region and internationally. It seeks to:

- work for the improvement of the image of Muslim women among Muslims and the community at large;
- promote educational initiatives to raise Muslim women's awareness of important and relevant issues;
- lobby to achieve social justice and empowerment of Australian Muslim women in society, especially in the workforce;
- campaign for the elimination of any form of violence against women and children; and
- work together with other women's organisations to share and exchange ideas and views.

It conducts workshops and seminars on issues of interest to Muslim women, and it develops and distributes educational material on issues such as child abuse, family harmony and the fostering of Muslim families.

Discussion groups for Australian Muslim women have also multiplied recently. Cyberspace provides a forum for women to discuss their personal, religious and family issues while remaining anonymous. Discussions about how to deal with abusive husbands, how to find a marriage partner, whether one should or should not wear the veil or headscarf, and drug problems and the delinquency of children are some of the many topics covered by these groups.

Lastly, it should be said that many Australian Muslim women experience discrimination from within the wider community, rather than from within the Muslim community itself. This is particularly the case when a major crisis occurs overseas involving a Muslim-majority country. During the Gulf War in the early 1990s, and following the events of September 11 in 2001, there was a marked rise in the experience of abuse reported by Muslims, particularly women who were identifiable because of their headscarf. This ranged from assault, to having scarves ripped from their heads, to being spat upon, intimidated and having obscenities shouted at them, among other things.

Generally speaking, women who wear the headscarf worry that they will experience subtle discrimination in the workplace. Others relate that they feel they are being 'spoken down to', as if they are not intelligent or cannot speak English.

13

PERCEPTIONS OF ISLAM AND MUSLIMS

It is perhaps in long-held European memories and myths that the portrayal of Islam in the Australian psyche has had its basis, particularly given that for over two hundred years Australia has been a country of migrants, the largest share of which comes from Europe and in particular the British Isles. Australia itself has not had any significant conflicts against a Muslim nation, with the exception of the country's involvement in the First World War as part of the British Empire. The Ottomans, who were Muslims, were allied with Germany and Australians fought against them in what is now Turkey. However, the conflict does not appear to have been portrayed as a religious war between Australian Christians and Muslims of the Ottoman Empire.

Australia also has a connection with Muslims via Indonesia, our neighbour to the north, and the largest Muslim country in the world. The largely Muslim Malaysia is another close neighbour. However, the relationship between Australia and these nations has not specifically been seen through a religious lens. This may be in line with the idea that Australians prefer to keep religion in the private domain. That is not to say that Australians are not ever religious; however, it is generally considered impolite to parade religion in public.

Nevertheless, certain world events have contributed to a shift in the level of negative discourse about Islam and furthered the widely held belief that Islam and Muslims are somehow associated with extremism, intolerance and violence. Examples of such events are as follows:

- The Iranian revolution of 1979 in which the Shah of Iran— one of America's closest allies—was overthrown, was one such event. The revolution was seen as reflecting a rise in Islamic fanaticism and fundamentalism, in particular an abhorrence of the West. Iranian hostility towards and depiction of the United States as the 'Great Satan' certainly provided a basis for this image. Although Iran was only one of more than 56 Muslim countries in the world, what was happening in Iran was generalised to Muslims everywhere.

- Another event contributing to the shift was the furore that erupted over Salman Rushdie's book *The Satanic Verses* in the late 1980s, when the Ayatollah Khomeini issued his infamous fatwa identifying Rushdie as an apostate who should be killed. The fatwa generated much debate in the Western world, including Australia. With book burnings occurring in Britain, Pakistan and Bangladesh, Islam was depicted at the time as fanatical, anti-modern, against freedom of speech—

the antithesis of the best Western liberal values. The fatwa was largely ignored by Muslims, and even condemned as un-Islamic, but despite this, Islam gained another score in its image as a violent, mediaeval, fanatical and aggressive faith.

- In some sections of Western media, the Arab–Israeli conflict is portrayed sometimes as a conflict between Jews and Arabs/Muslims. Arabs/Muslims are often portrayed as aggressive, violent, intolerant, fanatical, barbaric, uncivilised, murderous and bloodthirsty.

- The 1991 Gulf War became one of the most important factors in providing an association between Islam and violence. Several articles written by Australian journalists or reproduced from, among others, American and British media, managed to equate Saddam Hussein specifically with Islam and Muslims. Like the Khomeini's fatwa and the Arab–Israeli conflict, in some circles the Gulf War was seen as a battle between Islam and the West.

- As well, terrorist activities committed in the name of Islam, whether in the Middle East or in such places as the Philippines and Indonesia, provided further stimulus for a negative portrayal of Islam. Militant Muslim groups have been identified as responsible for, among other things, the murder of foreign tourists in Egypt; the first World Trade Center bombing in February 1993, which brought terrorism onto American home soil; the American embassy bombings in Kenya and Tanzania in August 1998; ongoing conflicts in Chechnya and Kashmir; sectarian violence between Christians and Muslims in Indonesia; the bombing of the warship *USS Cole* in in Yemen October 2000, the kidnapping of locals and tourists in the Philippines by Abu Sayyaf rebels and the bombing in Bali in October 2002. Violence conducted in the name of Islam, particularly targeting American or Western interests overseas, has meant a constant bombardment of news images associating Islam with violence from the Australian and Western media.

Possibly the most shocking example of an activity that cemented the connection between Islam and violence in the minds of many came on September 11, 2001 with the almost simultaneous bombings of the Twin Towers of the New York World Trade Center and the Pentagon in Washington, and the crash of a fourth hijacked commercial passenger jet in Pennsylvania. Linked to ex-Saudi millionaire Osama bin Laden and the al-Qaeda network, the events of September 11 again brought Islam to the forefront of the world's attention. Perhaps more clearly than through any event in the past, Islam was seen as providing a rationale for mass murder and terrorism, emphasised by bin Laden's rhetoric. This has deepened the perception in certain sections of the Australian community that Islam is a global menace and a threat to the 'free' world.

Both global and local events have contributed to the negative image of Islam and Muslims in general, and while there are many Australian journalists who have provided other voices, a significant section of media (particularly some of the tabloid newspapers and talk-back radio) focuses on a negative treatment of Islam. From early on, doubts about the allegiances of Muslims living in Australia have been raised each time there has been a crisis in world events involving Islam or Muslims. These suspicions—which arose even during the First World War, when there was a perception that Australian Muslims had prior loyalties to the Ottoman caliph—have appeared to grow stronger over the last decade of the twentieth century, despite the lack of any evidence from research on Muslim migration and settlement to support the view. Ignoring the fact that Australia is a multicultural and multi-religious society and that the Muslim community is extremely diverse, some influential commentators and even politicians have suggested that Australia should re-think its policy concerning Muslim migration.

This is based on the notion that Muslims are a single formidable mass whose ideas and values do not fit in Western society and conflict with basic Australian 'Judeo-Christian' values. During the late 1990s Australia's policies on Asian immigration came under the spotlight with Pauline Hanson and her One Nation party bringing national attention to the issue. In her maiden speech to parliament, Hanson claimed: 'I believe we are in danger of being swamped by Asians . . . They have their own culture and religion, form ghettos and do not assimilate.' While there was much outrage over her comments and her opinions on Reconciliation, the focus on Asian immigration highlighted questions about Muslims and their ability to integrate into Australian society.

 ## Garry: On being a Muslim and a scientist

I came to Islam just over 16 years ago. I have an enquiring mind and love learning, and I was surprised to find that Islam encourages this. The Qur'an invites its reader to consider and investigate the world around them. This resonates with my background in science. The Qur'an depicts Adam as being given knowledge by God. In a sense Adam was the first scientist. This contrasts with the biblical view of Adam falling from grace because he sought knowledge by eating from the forbidden tree.

I find no separation of the sacred and the secular in Islam. It provides a way of living life which makes every act, no matter how mundane, an act of worship if done with the right intention and in the correct manner. This gives a sense of spirituality to my life including my professional life. Seeing an exquisitely preserved organism which became extinct tens or hundreds of millions of years ago or coming to grips with a new concept in science can be, for me, a spiritual experience, an experience which compliments and reinforces the spirituality I feel while reading the Qur'an or performing the prayer.

While many would see becoming a Muslim as limiting your life and view of the world, I find that Islam has broadened my mind and given a dimension to my life that was previously lacking.

2001 A DIFFICULT YEAR FOR MUSLIMS IN AUSTRALIA

Boat people

In 2000-01, several conservative politicians used the issue of the 'boat people' (many of whom are Muslim) to advance their political fortune. The boat people issue was widely debated and discussed, and the federal government, sensing the unease within the Australian community about 'boat people' and 'asylum seekers', followed a hardline policy. This is despite the fact that the refugee problem Australia faces is very small compared with that of other developed countries. According to statistics issued by the Department of Immigration and Multicultural Affairs (DIMA) on 25 July 2000, the total number of boat people arriving in Australia from 1989 was only 8289. In the rhetoric over the boat people, they were demonised, labelled as 'queue jumpers' or as potential terrorists, and in the most bizarre case were even accused of throwing their children into the sea (the 'children overboard' affair). The fuelling of hatred against these boat people through such demonisation continued in certain sections of the Australian community. Given that many of the boat people were Muslims, their demonisation in the media was considered an indirect demonisation of Muslims.

Sydney gang rapes

In late July 2001, a sensational story hit the Australian press about a spate of gang rapes in Sydney. Several young men were charged with, and later found guilty of, a number of sexual assault offences. The New South Wales police identified the perpetrators as being Lebanese and Muslim, the victims as Caucasian. Statistics were used and manipulated by some commentators to justify the view that crime in the state is now largely an ethnic problem. This is despite the fact that, in the context of the debate on 'gang rapes' NSW Bureau of Crime

Statistics figures actually challenge the view that rape somehow exists mainly in the so-called 'ethnic' areas of Sydney.

This story led to a series of verbal attacks on Islam and Muslims. Muslim organisations reported an upsurge in hate mail, threats of rape of Muslim women and obscene phone calls and death threats, particularly in Sydney where these rapes occurred. One example of some of the statements made in the media and incidents in the wake of the 'gang rapes' are of a talk-back caller referring to Muslim women wearing a scarf: 'There will be— and I'm certainly not trying to inspire it here—massive vigilante reaction. I would not like to be walking down the road as a girl in that headdress.' A pregnant Muslim woman was assaulted at a tram-stop in inner Melbourne. The assailants subjected her to racial abuse before threatening to murder her if she didn't remove her hijab (headscarf).

Responding to this abuse, Muslims argued that Islam does not condone rape under any circumstances and that Islamic law is most strict on issues such as rape. If the perpetrators of this crime were Muslim, they did not follow their religion in this matter. In a response to the barrage of attacks on talk-back radio and from some media commentators, the Australian Muslim Public Affairs Committee (AMPAC), a Muslim advocacy group based in Melbourne, said:

> There can be absolutely no religious or moral justification whatsoever for rape. The Muslim community stands with the rest of Australia in expressing our absolute condemnation and repulsion as to what has taken place . . . We ask our fellow Australians to be just. It is imperative that people recognise

that the actions of these individuals do not represent either the beliefs or practices of Muslims, nor the religion itself. Rather, these acts are the acts of bestial individuals who obviously care little for the dictates of their supposed religion.[1]

September 11

September 11, 2001 was one of the most difficult days for Muslims in Australia. Soon after the terrorist attack on New York and Washington, a strong backlash against the Muslim community had begun. September 11 became just another reason why Muslims should be the target of death threats, fire bombings, hate mail and physical attacks. Those who were visibly Muslim, women in particular, were spat on, harassed, their scarves torn. A mosque in Brisbane was firebombed while several others received bomb threats. In Brisbane a bus carrying children from a Muslim school was stoned as it went by. A federal parliamentarian, Julia Irwin (ALP) spoke of reports of abuse:

> Those who incite hatred are not limited to one religion. In the past few days, I have been alarmed by reported incidents of terror against Muslims in Australia. There were reports of the attempted firebombing of a mosque. In my own electorate of Fowler, I have heard reports of Muslim women being spat upon and having scarves torn from their heads. If you think that is trivial, can you imagine a Catholic nun having her scarf torn from her head? We have seen students of Arabic origin verbally abused on a university campus. These are acts of hatred; they are acts of terror. They are minor in comparison

with the events of New York and Washington, but they must also be condemned. Until we realise that terrorism breeds on hatred and bigotry, until we realise that these faults are not limited to one religion, we will not be free from the threat of terrorism.[2]

Fortunately, such incidents were relatively few and only a very small minority within Australia behaved in this manner. The vast majority were sympathetic to the plight of the Muslim community here. Both the federal government and state governments throughout Australia were ready to assist the Muslim community in this difficult time. As in other states, police in Victoria, for instance, were working closely with the Islamic Council of Victoria to protect the community. On 17 September 2001, just one week after the attacks, many members of Federal Parliament expressed their feelings about the plight of the Muslim community. Senator Aden Ridgeway (Democrat) spoke for many Australians when he said:

> First and foremost, as Australians who pride ourselves on toler-
> ance and cultural diversity, we must condemn swiftly attacks
> by Australians on Muslim mosques, schools and businesses in
> the same manner in which we have condemned anti-Semitic
> comments in this country. Many of our Muslim and Arab
> friends, not unlike our Jewish friends, are Australian citizens
> and deserve our support at such a harrowing time.
> No Australian should feel under threat of abuse or be spat on
> or be stoned just because they are Muslim. We as Australians
> pride ourselves on democracy and its fundamental freedoms.
> Most of all, we must uphold the rule of law and guarantee

the rights and freedoms of every citizen in this nation without fear or favour.[3]

Within the Muslim community, individuals and community organisations were active in giving talks or interviews explaining what Islam is and distancing Muslim community from the terrorists.

RESPONSE OF AUSTRALIAN MUSLIMS

In the wake of the momentous events of 2001, Australian Muslims had to mount a defence against the barrage of criticism levelled against them, particularly in the tabloid newspapers and talk-back radio. It is fair to say that the leading newspapers in Australia, generally speaking, appear to have been balanced to a certain extent in their debate on Islam and violence and extremism. Space was given to those who were critical of Islam and Muslims as well as to those who wanted to show the 'Muslim' voice. Muslims who were engaged in the debate on talk-back radio, in their letters to the newspapers, articles, talks and lectures attempted to distance Islam from the accusations made against it as a religion of violence, fanaticism and extremism. They argued that violence in the name of religion is not a new phenomenon. In fact, all major religious traditions and ideologies that we know of, at one point or another have used violence and terrorism. Even today there are Hindu militants, Jewish militants, Christian militants; if we look at acts of violence perpetrated by Muslims, they are comparatively small despite the massive and prominent media coverage given to them. Australian Muslims have nothing to do with what Muslim terrorists do around the world, including the September 11 attacks on New York and Washington.

Muslims agree that every single community on earth has small minorities who do not fit into the bigger picture. For example, in Australia the vast majority of inhabitants are law-abiding citizens. It is only a very small minority who are criminals. The fact that there are such criminals within Australian society cannot be used to make the statement that the Australian community is criminal, bloodthirsty, murderous and violent. Perhaps a closer analogy lies with the Christian community. While there exist a small number of cults and extremist right-wing Christians who commit acts of violence, the overwhelming majority of Christians are peaceful, law-abiding citizens whose religion teaches them to treat others as they would wish to be treated themselves.

Whatever the reasons behind the actions of some militants in the Muslim world, Australian Muslims have no interest whatsoever in extremism, violence, killing, murder, suicide bombing and so on. They live normal lives and detest the association of Islam and Muslims with violence and aggression.

The doctrine of 'jihad' has also been a focus of the media, particularly after September 11. Jihad has been represented as the Islamic religious doctrine that justifies terror against the West. What the media has never discussed is that jihad is understood differently by Muslims around the world.

Literally, jihad means 'struggle'. This 'struggle' can be:

- to free oneself from sin, bad deeds, thoughts and words, or to purify oneself spiritually;

- to use one's abilities or skills to support causes considered 'pleasing' in the eyes of God, such as helping one's parents or relatives, or the needy and the disadvantaged, or doing something beneficial for the community;
- to defend one's homeland from outside aggression and invasion (this is usually carried out by the state or by the community as a whole, not by certain individuals or small groups).

Calls for jihad against the West are often made by those who are outside Australia and such calls have no audience in the mainstream Australian Muslim community. Australian Muslims argue that it is unfair to label all Muslims as adopting a view of jihad that is supported by militants and extremists elsewhere, and that Muslims in Australia have not adopted a militant interpretation of the doctrine. The statements made by the Australian Federation of Islamic Councils, state and territory Islamic councils, Islamic societies, imams and community leaders in relation to attacks against the West, such as September 11 and more recently the Bali bombing, all attest to this.

AUSTRALIAN MUSLIMS CHALLENGING THE NEGATIVE PORTRAYAL OF ISLAM

Australian Muslims have begun to challenge this onslaught against Islam and Muslims in the Australian media; however, at the time of writing there is no nationwide Muslim lobby which can muster the resources of the community to most effectively meet this challenge. In the past, individuals within the community have worked to counter negative stereotypes, and Australian converts to Islam have played a significant role in this effort. Because of their familiarity with the Australian system, its culture, values and language, they have been able to de-mystify some aspects of Islam which the media has tended to portray negatively. They have brought to light issues that are important in understanding the nature of conflicts among Muslims or between Muslims and members of other religious traditions.

In countering the stereotypical view of Islam and the negative portrayal of Islam and Muslims, Muslims are using a variety of media, from newsletters, newspapers, to radio and even television. Since the 1980s, Muslim community groups and individuals have been publishing regular newsletters, newspapers and magazines. These include *Australian Muslim News* (Sydney) of the Australian Federation of Islamic Councils (AFIC), *Australian Islamic Review* (Adelaide), *Crescent* (Brisbane), and *Azan Newsletter* of the Northern Territory. These often include articles on religious and social issues, as well as informing the community of services, facilities and upcoming events. In times of difficulty, these media outlets become tools for defending Muslims.

Local Muslim radio stations broadcasting 24 hours a day or for limited periods include 'Voice of Islam' in Sydney, the 'Bosnian Muslim Radio Program' and the Moroccan Program in South Australia. Radio stations in Victoria include 'Islamic Radio' and 'Iman Voice', and there are TV broadcasts on Channel 31. Muslim Community Radio, which is a multicultural and multilingual Islamic radio station based in Sydney, has been broadcasting to the Sydney Muslim community since 1995. Because Arabic is, according to statistics, the major ethnic language of communication among Muslims in Sydney, its broadcasts are mainly in Arabic and English, with some in other community languages.

More recently, Muslim individuals, groups, societies, councils and organisations have used the medium of the Internet to express their views and bring Muslims together. Whether locality based, or devoted to particular issues, websites and e-mail lists are playing a more significant role in uniting Muslim communities than the more traditional channels. The Internet is thus providing Muslims with an excellent tool for forming and uniting groups (often in cyberspace) as well as helping each other keep in touch. This type of interaction would not have been possible ten or fifteen years ago.

Australian Muslims acknowledge that not all Australians possess a paranoid view of Islam, and many groups, including Christian churches as well as journalists and media commentators, have come to the defence of Muslims. Sympathetic voices in the media, and groups committed to tolerance, have also provided alternative views. In the long term, it is most likely that cooperation between Muslims and other sections of the community will continue, particularly as Muslims become more involved with inter-faith and cross-cultural dialogues. The Muslim population in Australia is small, representing less than 1.5 per cent of the population. Because of this, it is vulnerable on many fronts and Muslims, as well as their non-Muslim fellow Australians, will need to find the resources to correct negative and misleading portrayals of Islam.

14

COMMITMENT TO FUNDAMENTAL AUSTRALIAN VALUES

Although Muslim communities in Australia have been growing and forming their own unique Australian identity since the beginnings of settlement, the perception that Islam and Muslims are somehow incapable of adapting to Australian values and life remains widespread. It is largely based on the idea that Islam is a religion which is against modernity and Western values, and that therefore Muslims in Australia are unable to adapt to their host culture. One commentator, Melanie Phillips, has neatly summarised the Western fear of Muslims, including in Australia:

> Muslims not only despise Western secular values as decadent, materialistic, corrupt and immoral. They do not accept the distinction between the spiritual and the temporal, the division which in Christian societies confines religion to the margins of everyday life. Instead, for Muslims, the whole of human life must represent a submission to God.

This means that they feel a duty to Islamicise the values of the surrounding culture. Since most of the mass immigration now convulsing Europe is composed of Muslims, it is therefore hardly surprising that anti-immigrant feeling is largely anti-Muslim feeling. The sheer weight of numbers, plus the refusal to assimilate to Western values, makes this an unprecedented crisis for Western liberalism. The crisis is forcing it to confront the fundamental questions of what constitutes a country, national identity and the very nature of a liberal society.[1]

One may ask, 'What are the secular values of the West that Muslims are claimed to despise so much?' If these values are the rule of law, democracy, human rights, equality, pluralism, a fair go for all, the truth of the matter is that Muslims around the world, including many in Australia, are often yearning for exactly these values. In fact, one reason why many Muslims migrate to the West is the very existence of these values. The fact that there are a few Muslims in Australia who may be against Western values does not justify the labelling of *all* Muslims as holding those views.

If what is referred to as Western secular values are values such as commercialisation of women's bodies (or, for that matter, men's bodies), licentiousness, drunkenness, gambling, alcohol or drug abuse, extreme individualism, family breakdowns, disrespect for the law, sexual harassment or nudity, it would be unfair to attribute all of these and similar values to all Westerners or all Australians and to say that these are the secular values we cherish and on which Australian society is based. Of course, in Australia, there are those who may cherish these values, and they have every right to do so, but there are plenty of others who reject them. If Muslims reject these values they are not unique; in fact, they would be in agreement with a significant number of Australians who practise any number of religions, Christanity among them. It would be an insult to the large number of Australians who share with Muslims, Christians, Jews, Buddhists and others the same abhorrence of some or all of these values to attribute these values to them.

In Australia, even the most traditionalist Muslims function perfectly well within Australian society. They participate in the election of the government (and do not have a moral objection to voting for a non-Muslim), interact with various institutions within the society, live next door to people who are not Muslim, shop at supermarkets or in stores that are run by non-Muslims, work for non-Muslims, employ non-Muslims in their businesses, and earn their livelihood just like other ordinary Australians do. Muslims do not seem to hold demonstrations in Australian cities to get rid of bars, nightclubs, brothels, massage parlours, casinos, breweries and wineries, discos, nudist beaches or the Gay and Lesbian Mardi Gras. Muslims do not distribute flyers calling for an uprising against such things. Like many other Australians, they may not agree with them, but they do not try to get rid of them either. They have adopted the view that Australia is a place where different people from different backgrounds, religious traditions and belief systems have different views on these issues. Those who want to engage in certain practices and hold cetain values should have the freedom to do so. Similarly, those who do not want to adopt them should also have the right not to do so. The fact of the matter is, these things exist in most Muslim countries and Muslims are used to living with them. Australia is not the first place they have seen a brothel, a night club, a casino or a bar. Most Muslims in Australia have adopted the approach of 'live and let live'; it is not the Muslim's duty to change Australian society.

Related to this issue is the argument advanced by some in the West that Muslims want to change the nature of Western liberal society and convert it to some form of 'Islamic theocracy'. Thus, France could become the Islamic Republic of France or Australia the Islamic Republic of Australia. Again, there may be Muslims who believe that such a thing is possible; indeed, that it is their duty to contribute to the 'Islamisation' of the world. But this does not seem to be a general characteristic of Muslims in the West or in Australia. It may be the dream of a few Muslims, just like there are some Christians who dream of 'Christianising' the world and bringing the 'Kingdom of God' to all. Most, if not all, religious groups have their fair share of such dreamers. Muslims are no different.

MUSLIMS' COMMITMENT TO FUNDAMENTAL AUSTRALIAN VALUES

The fundamental values on which Australian society and institutions are based include egalitarianism, rule of law, parliamentary democracy, respect for human rights, freedom of expression, equality of the sexes, multiculturalism, religious pluralism and English as a national language. The question usually asked is, 'Are Australian Muslims committed to these values?'

It is difficult to put forward a generalised view with regard to 'Muslim commitment' to these fundamental values. Many factors seem to influence a person's (of any religious background) commitment to these values. These factors may include length of residence in Australia, the degree of acceptance of the person by the wider community, the economic and other opportunities available, the degree of mobility to move to a 'home' country somewhere else, and the religious orientation of the person. It is the combined effect of all or most of these factors that seems to determine whether a person has a strong positive commitment or a strong negative commitment to these fundamental values.

Despite this, many commentators who argue that Muslims in general are hostile to 'Western' (or Australian) values, usually focus on religion as the only determining factor arguing that Islam is incompatible with 'Western' values. While there are many Muslims who focus on certain negative aspects of Western societies and compare those aspects with positive aspects of Muslim societies and assert that Islam is not compatible with 'Western' values, there are many more Muslims who argue that such a superficial comparison is misleading and simplistic. For the latter, there are many Western values that have been adopted by Muslims, and the West has much to offer to Muslims. They also believe that there are certain Islamic values from which the West can benefit. For them, both Islam (i.e. Muslim societies) and the West are complementary rather than antagonistic. Again, there is no one view on this issue among Muslims. While some

Muslims love to hate the West and Western values, plenty of other Muslims do the very opposite. Adoption of the so-called Western values even among the political Islamists (who, based on their rhetoric, should have been among the most ardent opponents of such values) is well known. Examples include the emphasis in Islamist discourse on human rights, democracy and freedom of expression. The anti-Western rhetoric among some Muslims where that exists, in many cases, is nothing more than a relic of the anti-colonial sentiments among Muslims, which has little to do with religion.

In this context, it is important to note that, as has already been pointed out in this book, Muslims' approaches to Islam can range from extreme 'liberalism' to extreme traditionalism. It is a continuum and therefore it is more fruitful to find where each person fits on the continuum. In relation to the commitment to fundamental Australian values, it is possible to suggest that the religious orientation of Muslims can be classified as follows.

Traditionalists: Two groups of traditionalists exist.

(a) Those committed to a pre-modern conception of Islamic law (shari'a) and believe that, in Australia, Muslims are functioning in a non-Islamic political and legal environment, which they find therefore highly problematic. Because of this environment, they may feel that they are unable to function fully as Muslims in Australia.

(b) Those who are mainly interested in following traditionalist positions in the areas of worship and ritual and are not overly concerned with the broad political and legal environment. Their main interest is to function as practising Muslims in their personal life and in areas such as rituals. They have no particular difficulties in adjusting to the Australian environment, and therefore to fundamental Australian values.

Neo-Revivalists: These see it as their duty to 'revive' and 'reform' the Muslim community (*umma*) through the propagation of the religion, and 'Islamise' the institutions and systems in the society wherever possible, with particular focus on Muslim-majority countries. Thus in such countries, neo-Revivalists are keen to Islamise the political, economic, legal and educational systems there, as they have attempted in Pakistan and Sudan. With regard to the West and Western values two groups seem to exist among neo-Revivalists:

(a) Those for whom most Western values, ideas and institutions are inherently non-Islamic and even anti-Islamic. They show a high degree of hostility to the West and 'Western values' in their rhetoric. They are often ideologically linked to the thought of anti-Western neo-Revivalist thinkers of the twentieth century,

(b) Those who are critical of the West and 'Western values' without showing the hostility of the first group. Their focus is on 'reforming' Muslim societies from within and they are moderate in their assessment of what can or cannot be done. They tend to be more pragmatic and have no particular difficulty in living in the West and adopting many of the Western values, while remaining faithful to Islam.

Neo-Modernists: Generally speaking, these have a much more relaxed attitude to new ideas, values and institutions. They are often quite happy to reinterpret certain Islamic ideas to fit in with modern developments without compromising on fundamental core values and practices of Islam. For them, there is no inherent conflict between Islam and Western values as such; one has to look carefully at what the specific points of comparison are before making any judgments about the existence or otherwise of the assumed conflict. Many Australian Muslims fall into this category.

Liberals: These include both practising and non-practising Muslims who often have a rather secular outlook. For them, Islam is essentially a religion that focuses on the relationship between an individual and God. For these Muslims, it is simplistic to talk about the existence of a conflict between Islam and the so-called Western values. Their position is not too far from that of the neo-Modernists. A very large number of Muslims in Australia would fit into this category.

The above indicates that a relatively small section of Muslims in Australia is likely to be hostile to the West and Western values, and by extension to fundamental Australian values. These Muslims are likely to belong to the Traditionalist (a) and neo-Revivalist (a) categories. While both have some presence in Australia, they cannot be said to represent the vast majority of Muslims. For the rest, living in Australia is as normal as living in any other 'Muslim' country. In fact, living in Australia may be preferable to living in some of the so-called Muslim countries, where personal freedom (even religious freedom), democracy, human rights, or the rule of law often do not exist.

In a sense, it is the fundamental Australian values (call them Western liberal values) that perhaps attract the vast majority of Muslims to Australia.

While there are some Muslims who are afraid of losing their ethnic and cultural identity in Australia, there are many more who are confident that they can be Australians as well as Muslims, and who believe there is no conflict between the two. For the vast majority of Muslims, there is no problem in being a fully functioning and contributing member of Australian society while remaining faithful to the core values, ideas and institutions of Islam.

Over the past 1400 years, Islam and Muslims have managed to adapt to a huge variety of cultures and peoples from every corner of the world. This process is still at work in Muslim communities living in the West, including in Australia. The concepts of democracy, the nation-state, human rights, the rule of law and equality of the sexes have all become part and parcel of Muslims' lives in these communities, despite there being small pockets of resistance to these concepts among Muslims.

As has already been pointed out, Muslim communities in Australia are largely composed of migrants from various parts of the Muslim world who bring with them ideas, values, institutions and practices of their local cultures, and therefore Muslims in Australia do not form a single homogeneous community; in fact, they make up many different communities from various parts of the world. Their attitudes, behaviours, ideas, values and perspectives reflect the sorts of cultures from which they originally came. But over time, many aspects of their original cultures are modified or forfeited in place of new attitudes, ideas, values and practices. Those who are committed and practising Muslims retain the core of Islam, which is composed of a number of basic beliefs, ideas, practices, views and institutions.

In Australia, there is no inherent contradiction between being Christian and Australian, or being Jewish and Australian. Likewise, there is no contradiction between being Muslim and Australian.

Children of migrants adopt the ideas, values and institutions of the host country and become born-and-bred Australians. They go to local schools and learn the standard curricula. Their interests, the television programs they watch, the games they play, the places they visit, their neighbours, their sporting interests and heroes, are Australian and related to local Australian culture rather than to the culture of their parents. In fact, the home culture of their parents can be extremely foreign and difficult to cope with, especially if that home culture is markedly different.

Migrant Muslims and their children can both remain committed to Islam and function within the broader Australian society and the fundamental values upon which the society is based. It does not mean that every single cultural trait will be rejected and a new one adopted; rather, Muslims may retain their commitment to the religion, but also vote for the political party of their choice; take part in community life, contribute to the economy, buy their homes in average neighbourhoods and live essentially 'normal' lives. Of course, there will always be a minority who wish to distinguish themselves from the mainstream. Such minorities exist in all cultures and communities, and are not simply a Muslim phenomenon.

Zohal Yussuf:
Being a refugee

Whenever my mum mentions how much my family suffered in Eritrea and how they had to run for their lives, I realise how blessed I am to be here. I was actually born in Sudan and we had to hide our Eritrean identity and pretend we were Sudanese so that we wouldn't have our home taken away from us. Whenever I watch the news and see people across the world that are starving or have nowhere to sleep, I thank God for being here in Australia.

I arrived in Melbourne in March 1995 with my mum and brother, although my dad is still overseas. I haven't seen him since I was twelve. Currently he is working in Saudi Arabia to support us and his sisters (my aunts), but God willing, we hope he will be able to settle here at the end of this year so that my family can be reunited.

It didn't take me long to get used to Aussie culture, particularly because Islam teaches me to accept diversity, and I believe that Australia is an example of how people from different regions and cultures can exist in peace and harmony. As an Australian Muslim, I like to look at the similarities rather than the difference, so I am quite happy to share lunch with my Jewish and Christian friends. The generosity and warm welcome I received from the Australian people will remain a debt which God commands me to pay back, and I look forward to an even better future for this country with more understanding and tolerance.

EPILOGUE

While the Muslim presence in Australia dates back as far as the mid-nineteenth century, it was severely curtailed with the beginning of the Commonwealth of Australia and the White Australia Policy. Muslims then either assimilated into the wider Australian society or left for their home countries. Very few remained as practising Muslims. It was in the 1960s that the Muslim population in Australia began to grow.

The decades of the 1960s to the 1990s may be considered a relatively calm and positive period for Muslims in Australia. The growth of Islam was fostered by multiculturalism and the abolition of the White Australia Policy, the influx of Muslim students, the non-discriminatory immigration policy which brought Muslims from a variety of backgrounds, the establishment of Islamic organisations (both local and national), the development of a series of important Islamic institutions such as schools, mosques and Islamic centres, and the increasing interest in Islam from Australians of European background. Given all of this, the consolidation of Islam as an essential part of the religious fabric of Australia is likely to continue despite the setbacks seen since the late 1990s.

The non-contentious presence of Muslims in Australia was rudely shaken by several events from the late 1990s onwards. The rise of Hansonism, buttressed by politicians on both sides catering to its supporters, the problem of asylum seekers (many of whom are Muslim) and the harsh stand taken by the federal government in dealing with them, and finally the momentous events of September 11, have shaken the core of the Muslim presence in Australia. While Hansonism is not directed particularly at Muslims, its anti-immigration stance has fuelled antipathy towards the seemingly different migrant: that is, the non-European, including Muslims. The indirect portrayal of asylum seekers of Muslim background as potential terrorists or at best untrustworthy, in the wake of September 11, has provided further fuel to anti-Muslim feeling. Further inflaming the situation are certain small sections of the media, particularly within the tabloids and talk-back radio, reminding Australians of the 'Muslim menace' right here in the middle of Australian society. In the post-September 11 period, one of the areas highlighted by a number of Australian commentators was that Muslims in general have a 'hostile attitude' towards the West, portray it as morally bankrupt and decadent, and look down on the West in general, and, by implication, Australia. Muslims are also portrayed as working to 'conquer' the West by changing Western values, institutions and systems to ones that are Islamic. In this,

Islam and the West are pictured as two homogeneous entities on a collision course, with Muslims and Islam seen as a fundamental threat to the existence of Western liberal values, and thus Muslims in Australia are 'an enemy within'.

Despite this gloom, the vast majority of Australians do not seem to take a hostile view of Muslims as such. At all levels of Australian society, there is a remarkable degree of tolerance, if not acceptance, of Muslims as part of this society. Australia's legal framework provides for added safeguards. Australia remains among the most tolerant and hospitable societies in the Western world for Muslims. However, one of the most important challenges for Muslim leaders in this new environment is to allay the fears of ordinary Australians that Muslims are indeed anti-Western, anti-Australian and not truly part of Australian society. Part of the challenge is to confront and explain the negative nature of such views. Although many Muslims, as individuals, have attempted this, their efforts have been sporadic and ad hoc, and much needs to be done in this area on a systematic and strategic basis. There is a duty on the part of Muslim leaders (both religious and lay) to explain these issues, clarify them to the broader Australian community, and present a balanced view. As part of the Muslim response, Australian Muslims will also have to build closer links to other religious communities in Australia, in order to work with them on issues such as religious harmony, humanitarian concerns and social issues. Leaders of the Muslim communities will have to find ways of de-emphasising ethnic/national distinctions and emphasising religious/Australian identification, leading to further consolidation of

Australian Muslims into an umma (community) whose loyalty lies to Australia, rather than to any other nation somewhere else.

In order to deal with many of the challenges Australian Muslims face, it is important that they, in the immediate future, develop a religious leadership that is trained in classical Islamic disciplines, but is at the same time at home with modern issues and is thoroughly familiar with Australian society, culture and history. Such leaders must be able to communicate in English in a community more and more members of which are Muslims who were born and grew up in Australia within an Australian ethos. Such a leadership must be able to present Islamic norms and values in an understandable and relevant form to the increasing number of Australian Muslims for whom the idea of being Australian should not conflict with being Muslim. Negotiating this will not be easy, but those who are truly both Muslim and Australian can accomplish this task.

Islam in Australia, although it represents the many manifestations of Islam around the world, is now being shaped by the prevailing values, norms and practices of Australian society. Values fundamental to Australian society are now being accommodated into what is considered to be Islam. New generations of Australian-born Muslims are the most ardent proponents of such a view. For them, it is an Islam that is comfortable with these values which will remain meaningful and relevant to their life in Australia.

GLOSSARY

A note on the use of italics for non-English words
Arabic and other non-English words are italicised in the first
instance only.

adhan: call to prayer, five times a day
akhlaq: Islamic norms of behaviour and etiquette
Allah: God
al-Masjid al-Aqsa: Aqsa Mosque in Jerusalem
al-Masjid al-Nabawi: Mosque of the Prophet Muhammad in
    Medina
'aqiqa: Islamic naming ceremony
Ash'ari school: one of the theological schools in Islam
Asr: the afternoon prayer
Aws: one of the two Arab tribes in Medina at the time of the
    Prophet
Aya: a verse of the Qur'an
Ayesha: one of the wives of the Prophet

Bukhari: Sunni scholar of hadith. His collection of hadith is considered the most authentic collection by Sunni Muslims

du'a: supplication

Eid: day of festivities. There are two Eids in Islam: Eid al-Fitr and Eid al-Ad ha

Eid al-Ad ha: Eid that occurs during the pilgrimage time, on the 10th day of Dhu al-Hijja (the twelfth month in the Islamic calendar)

Eid al-Fitr: Eid that occurs immediately after the month of Ramadan (month of fasting), on the 1st of Shawwal, the tenth month of the Islamic calendar

Fatima: one of the daughters of the Prophet Muhammad

Fajr: dawn; the dawn prayer

fatwa: a response by a scholar of Islamic law to a question related to Islamic law

hadith: sayings and deeds of the Prophet Muhammad as documented by his followers

halal: permissible under Islamic law

Hanafi school: one of the legal schools in Islam

Hanbali school: one of the legal schools in Islam

hajja: a female Muslim who has performed the hajj (pilgrimage)

haji: a male Muslim who has performed the hajj (pilgrimage)

hajj: pilgrimage to Mecca

hijab: veil; headscarf

hijra: migration of the Prophet Muhammad from Mecca to Medina in 622

Ibadi school: one of the religio-political/theological/legal schools in Islam

Iblis: Satan

iftar: breaking of fast at sunset

imam: a leader; a leader in prayer

Injil: Gospel

'Isha: the prayer at night, performed an hour or so after sunset

Islam: the name of the religion preached by the Prophet Muhammad

Ja'fari school: a Shi'i school of law

Jibril: Gabriel

jihad: struggle

Jumada al-Thaniya: 6th month in Islamic calendar

Jumada al-Ula: 5th month in Islamic calendar

Ka'ba: a cube-shaped building in the centre of the Grand Mosque in Mecca, the holiest place for Muslims on earth

Karbala: a sacred place for Shi'i Muslims, in Iraq

Khazraj: one of the two Arab tribes in Medina at the time of the Prophet

khutba: sermon; Friday sermon

Laylat al-Qadr: 'Night of Power', believed to be in the month of Ramadan

Maghrib: sunset; sunset prayer

Maliki school: one of the Sunni legal schools in Islam

masjid: mosque; place of prayer

Masjid al-Haram: Grand Mosque in Mecca

mufti: a Muslim scholar of Islamic law who can issue Islamic legal opinions

Muharram: the first month of Islamic calendar

Muslim Brotherhood: a neo-Revivalist movement established by Hasan al-Banna in the early twentieth century in Egypt

Mu'tazili school: a theological school in Islam

Qur'an: the Holy Scripture of Islam, revealed to Prophet Muhammad between 610 and 632, in Arabic

Quraysh: the main tribe in Mecca at the time of the Prophet Muhammad, to which he belonged

Rabi' al-Awwal: the 3rd month of the Islamic calendar

Rabi' al-Thani: the 4th month of the Islamic calendar

Rajab: the 7th month of the Islamic calendar

Ramadan: the 9th month of the Islamic calendar, the month of fasting

sadaqa: charity

Safar: the 2nd month of the Islamic calendar

Sha'ban: the 8th month of the Islamic calendar

shahada: Muslim confession of faith

shari'a: Islamic law

Shawwal: the 10th month of the Islamic calendar

Shi'a: an Islamic religio-political/theological grouping

Sufism: a movement within Islam that emphasises Islamic spirituality

Sunni: the mainstream Muslim community to which approximately 85 per cent of the Muslim population of the world belongs

suhur: meal taken before dawn in Ramadan

Sura: chapter of the Qur'an

Taj al-Din al-Hilali: imam based in Sydney

tarawih: a prayer performed during Ramadan, after the 'Isha prayer

umra: lesser pilgrimage in Islam

Yathrib: name of Medina at the time of the Prophet

zakat: obligatory charity in Islam

Zuhr: noon; noon prayer

SELECTED BIBLIOGRAPHY

Abdel-Halim, Aziza (1989) *Meeting the Needs of Muslim Students in the Australian Education System*, Sydney, Self-published

Abu Duhou, Ibtisam and Teese, Richard (1992) *Education, Workforce and Community Participation of Arab Australians: Egyptians, Lebanese, Palestinians and Syrians*, AGPS, Canberra

Akbarzadeh, Shahram (2001) 'Unity or Fragmentation?' in Abdullah Saeed and Shahram Akbarzadeh (eds) *Muslim Communities in Australia*, UNSW Press, Sydney

Asmar, Christine (1992) 'The Arab-Australian Experience' in Murray Goot and Rodney Tiffin (eds) *Australia's Gulf War*, Melbourne University Press, Melbourne, pp. 57–81

——(2001) 'A Community on Campus: Muslim Students in Australian Universities' in Abdullah Saeed and Shahram Akbarzadeh (eds) *Muslim Communities in Australia*, UNSW Press, Sydney

Ata, A.W. (1984) 'Moslem-Arab Portrayal in the Australian Press and in School Textbooks', *Australian Journal of Social Issues*, 19(1)

Bentley, Peter, Blombery, Tricia and Hughes, Philip (1992) *Faith Without the Church: Nominalism in Australian Christianity*, Christian Research Association, Melbourne

Berns McGown, Rima (1999) *Muslims in the Diaspora*, University of Toronto Press, Toronto

Bouma, Gary (1994) *Mosques and Muslim Settlement in Australia*, Bureau of Immigration, Multicultural and Population Research, Canberra

——(1995a) *Religious Tolerance in Australia*, World Conference on Religion and Peace, Melbourne

——(1995b) 'The Emergence of Religious Plurality in Australia, a Multicultural Society', *Sociology of Religion*, 56, pp. 285–302

——(1997a) 'The Religious Settlement of Islam in Australia', *Social Compass*, 44, pp. 71–82

——(ed.) (1997b) *Many Religions, All Australian: Religious Settlement, Identity and Cultural Diversity*, Christian Research Association, Melbourne

——(1999a) 'From Hegemony to Pluralism: Managing Religious Diversity in Modernity and Post-modernity', *Australian Religious Studies Review*, 12(3), pp. 7–27

——(ed.) (1999b) *Managing Religious Diversity: From Threat to Promise*, Australian Association for the Study of Religions, Sydney

Bouma, Gary, Daw, Joan and Munawwar, Riffat (2001) 'Muslims Managing Religious Diversity' in Abdullah Saeed and Shahram Akbarzadeh (eds) *Muslim Communities in Australia*, UNSW Press, Sydney

Brasted, Howard V. (1997) 'The Politics of Stereotyping. Western Images of Islam', *Manushi*, 98, January-February

——(2001) 'Contested Representations in Historical Perspective: Images of Islam and the Australian Press 1950–2000' in Abdullah Saeed and Shahram Akbarzadeh (eds) *Muslim Communities in Australia*, UNSW Press, Sydney

Buckley, Siddiq (1987) 'The Struggle for Nur', *Insight*, 2(1)

Buckley, Silma (1991) *Bridges of Light: The Struggle of an Islamic Private School in Australia*, The Muslim Service Association, New South Wales

Carey, Hilary (1996) *Believing in Australia: A Cultural History of Religions*, Allen & Unwin, Sydney

Champion, Daryl (1994) 'Muslims and the Media in Australia', *Journal of Arabic, Islamic and Middle East Studies*, 1(2)

Clark, C.M.H. (1955) *Select Documents in Australian History 1851–1900*, Angus & Robertson, Melbourne

Cleland, Bilal (2001a) 'The History of Muslims in Australia' in Abdullah Saeed and Shahram Akbarzadeh (eds) *Muslim Communities in Australia*, UNSW Press, Sydney

——(2001b) *The Muslims in Australia: A Brief History*, Islamic Council of Victoria, Melbourne

Cunningham, Stuart and Turner, Graeme (eds) (1997) *The Media in Australia*, Allen & Unwin, Sydney

Deen, Hanifa (1995) *Caravanserai: Journey among Australian Muslims*, Allen & Unwin, Sydney

Department of Education, Training and Youth Affairs (DETYA) (2000) *Students 1999: Selected Higher Education Statistics*, AGPS, Canberra

Dietze, Erich von (1997) 'Halal Food on Curtin's Bentley Campus', *Journal of the Australian and New Zealand Student Services Association*, 9 April, pp. 58–65

Donohoue-Clyne, Irene (1998) 'Cultural Diversity and the Curriculum: The Muslim experience in Australia', *European Journal of Intercultural Studies*, 9 (3) pp. 279–89

Donohoue-Clyne, Irene (1999) 'Educating Muslim Children: An Inter-cultural challenge for Teachers' in K. Häkkinen (ed.) *Innovative Approaches to Intercultural Education*, Continuing Education Centre, University of Jyväskylä, Jyväskylä, Finland

——(2001) 'Educating Muslim Children in Australia' in Abdullah Saeed and Shahram Akbarzadeh (eds) *Muslim Communities in Australia*, UNSW Press, Sydney

Family Law Council (1994) *Female Genital Mutilation: A Report to the Attorney-General*, Commonwealth of Australia, Canberra

Fitzpatrick, Brian (1969) *The British Empire in Australia 1834–1939*, Macmillan, Melbourne

Fuller, Basil (1975) *The Ghan: The Story of the Alice Springs Railway*, Rigby, Adelaide

Hage, Ghassan (1991) 'Racism, Multiculturalism and the Gulf War', *Arena*, 96, Spring

Hogan, Michael (1987) *The Sectarian Strand: Religion in Australian History*, Allen & Unwin, Sydney

Hugo, Graeme (1992) *Atlas of the Australian People: New South Wales, 1986 Census*, AGPS, Canberra

Humphrey, Michael (1984) *Family, Work and Unemployment: A Study of Lebanese Settlement in Sydney*, DIEA, Canberra

——(1987) 'Community, Mosque and Ethnic Politics', *Australian and New Zealand Journal of Sociology*, 23(2), July, pp. 233–45

——(1988) 'Muslim Lebanese' in James Jupp (ed.) *The Australian People*, Angus & Robertson, Sydney, pp. 677–80

——(1989) 'Is this a Mosque-Free Zone? Islam and the State in Australia', *Migration Monitor*, 12, January, pp. 12–17

——(1991) 'Islam, Immigration and the State: Religion in Australia' in Alan W. Black (ed.) *Religion in Australia. Sociological Perspectives*, Allen & Unwin, Sydney

——(1998) *Islam, Multiculturalism and Transnationalism: From the Lebanese Diaspora*, IB Tauris, London and New York

——(2000) 'Globalisation and Arab Diasporic Identities: The Australian Arab Case', *Bulletin of the Royal Institute for Inter-Faith Studies*, 2 (1), pp. 1–18

——(2001) 'An Australian Islam? Religion in the Multicultural City' in Abdullah Saeed and Shahram Akbarzadeh (eds) *Muslim Communities in Australia*, UNSW Press, Sydney

Humphrey, Michael and Shepard, William (2000) 'Australia and New Zealand' in David Westerlund and Ingvar Svanberg (eds) *Islam Outside the Arab World*, Curzon, Richmond, pp. 278–94

Hussain, Jamila (2001) 'Family Law and Muslim Communities' in Abdullah Saeed and Shahram Akbarzadeh (eds) *Muslim Communities in Australia*, UNSW Press, Sydney

Ierodiaconou, Mary-Jane (1995) 'Listen to Us: Female Genital Mutilation, Feminism and the Law in Australia', *Melbourne University Law Review*, 20 (2), pp. 562–87

Inglis, Christine and Manderson, Lenore (1991) 'Turkish Immigrants in Australia' in Margaret Gibson and John Ogbu (eds) *Minority Status and Schooling: A Comparative Study of Immigrants and Involuntary Minorities*, Garland Publishing Inc, New York

Inglis, Christine, Elley, Joy and Manderson, Lenore (1992) *Making Something of Myself: Educational Attainment and Social and Economic Mobility of Turkish-Australian Young People*, AGPS, Canberra

Johns, A. (1997) 'Muslim Communities in Australia: An Opportunity for Inter-faith Conciliation', *Hamard Islamicus*, 20 (3), pp. 7–21

Jones, Mary Lucille (ed.) (1993) *An Australian Pilgrimage: Muslims in Australia from the Seventeenth Century to the Present*, Victoria Press, Melbourne

Kalam, A. (1988) 'Primary Islamic Education: Essential for All Muslim Children', *Insight*, 3 (1)

Kamalkhani, Zahra (2001) 'Recently Arrived Muslim Refugee Women Coping with Settlement' in Abdullah Saeed and Shahram Akbarzadeh (eds) *Muslim Communities in Australia*, UNSW Press, Sydney

Lyng, J. (1935) *Non-Britishers in Australia: Influence on Population and Progress*,

Melbourne University Press in association with Oxford University Press, Melbourne

Mackie, F. (1983) *Structure, Culture and Religion in the Welfare of Muslim Families: Study of Immigrant Turkish and Lebanese men and Women and their Families Living in Melbourne*, DIEA, Canberra

Macknight, Charles Campbell (1976) *The Voyage to Marege*, Melbourne University Press, Melbourne

Markus, Andrew (1994) *Australian Race Relations 1788–1993*, Allen & Unwin, Sydney

Martin, Jean (1972) *Community and Identity: Refugee Groups in Adelaide*, Australian National University Press, Canberra

Mograby, Abdallah (1985) 'Muslim Migration and Settlement: The Australian Experience', *Islam in Australia*, Middle East Research and Information Section, NSW Anti-Discrimination Board, Sydney

Mubarak, Fatheena (1997) 'Muslim Women and Religious Identification: Women and the Veil', in Gary Bouma (ed.) *Many Religions, All Australian: Religious Settlement, Identity and Cultural Diversity*, Christian Research Association, Melbourne

Munawar, Riffat (1997) 'Intergenerational Cultural Difference Among Muslim Women in Wollongong', MA Thesis, Sociology Department, University of Wollongong, Wollongong

Nebhan, Katy (2000) 'Strategic Representations: Australian Muslims' Critique of the Fundamentalist Discourse' in R. Walker, K. Brass and J. Byron (eds) *Anatomies of Violence: An Interdisciplinary Investigation*, Post-graduate Arts Research Centre and the Research Institute for Humanities and Social Sciences, University of Sydney, Sydney

Omar, Wafia and Allen, Kirsty (1997) *The Muslims in Australia*, AGPS, Canberra

Onley, Norma (1989) *Migration and Women's Religious Experience*, Occasional Paper, No. 17, The Centre for Multicultural Studies, University of Wollongong, Wollongong

Penman, D. (1987) 'Religions in Australia. Can they Cope with Multiculturalism?', *Journal of International Studies*, 8, pp. 55–56

Pittaway, Eileen (1991) *Refugee Women—Still at Risk in Australia, A Study of the First Two Years of Resettlement in the Sydney Metropolitan Area*, AGPS, Canberra

Reese, Trevor R. (1964) *Australia in the Twentieth Century*, F.W. Cheshire, Melbourne

Saeed, Abdullah (2001) 'The Muslim Community Cooperative of Australia as an Islamic Financial Service Provider' in Abdullah Saeed and Shahram Akbarzadeh (eds) *Muslim Communities in Australia*, UNSW Press, Sydney

Saeed, Abdullah and Akbarzadeh, Shahram (eds) (2001) *Muslim Communities in Australia*, UNSW Press, Sydney

Sims, Peter C. (1987) *The Norfolk Settlers of Norfolk Island and Van Diemen's Land*, Quoiba, Tasmania

Stevens, Christine (1989) *Tin Mosques and Ghantowns: A History of Afghan Cameldrivers in Australia*, Oxford University Press, Melbourne

Sydney University Muslim Student Association (SUMSA) (2000) 'Requirements for Muslim Students', Unpublished report submitted to the University of Sydney, May

The Hon Mr Justice Woodward Commissioner (1982) *Report of the Royal Commission into Australian Meat Industry*, AGPS, September, Canberra

Wright, Reg (1986) *The Forgotten Generation of Norfolk Island and Van Diemen's Land*, Library of Australian History, Sydney

Yasmeen, Samina (2001) 'Settlement Needs of Muslim Women in Perth: A Case Study' in Abdullah Saeed and Shahram Akbarzadeh (eds) *Muslim Communities in Australia*, UNSW Press, Sydney

ENDNOTES

Chapter 1

1. Of the common era.
2. Bilal Cleland, *The Muslims in Australia: A brief history*, Islamic Council of Victoria, 2002, p. 6
3. Abdul Khaliq Fazal, 'Afghans' in James Jupp, *The Australian People*, Cambridge University Press, Cambridge, 2001, pp. 164–5
4. Michael Humphrey, 'Muslim Lebanese' in James Jupp, *The Australian People*, Cambridge University Press, Cambridge, 2001, pp. 564–7
5. Hurriyet Babacan, 'Turks' in James Jupp, *The Australian People*, Cambridge University Press, Cambridge, 2001, pp. 709–16
6. Centre for Immigration and Multicultural Studies (ANU), 'Bosnians', in James Jupp, *The Australian People*, Cambridge University Press, Cambridge, 2001, pp. 186–7
7. Riaz Hassan, 'Pakistanis' in James Jupp, *The Australian People*, Cambridge University Press, Cambridge, 2001, pp. 615–6
8. Janet Penny and Tuti Gunawan, 'Indonesian' in James Jupp, *The Australian People*, Cambridge University Press, Cambridge, 2001, pp. 439–41

Chapter 2

1. www.ii.uib.no/~georg/alt/rpg/ars/rules/ArsArabica/node39.html

Chapter 7

1. Khurram Murad, 'What does Eid celebrate again and again? God's bounty and His mercy' <http://www.jamaat.org/islam/eid.html> Downloaded 18 October 2002

2. www.gallipolimosque.org.au

Chapter 9

1. Compass Program, 'The Sheikh of Melbourne', ABC TV, Sunday May 6 2001 <http://www.abc.net.au/compass/s287380.htm> Downloaded 18 October 2002

Chapter 10

1. *Taqwa'ul Islam: International Online Islamic Magazine*, 'Halal Food Awareness' <http://majlis.freeyellow.com/halal1.htm> Downloaded 18 October 2002

2. Islamic Council of Queensland, *Healthcare Providers' Handbook on Muslim Patients* <http://www.health.qld.gov.au/hssb/hou/islamgde.pdf> Downloaded 18 October 2002

Chapter 13

1. AMPC, 'Rapists rape in spite of Islam, not because of it', <http://www.muslimaffairs.com.au/articles/Rape.htm> Download 18 October 2002

2. Statements of Federal politicians made on the opening of parliament (17/9/2001). Posted on the website of AMPAC 'News; Statements of Australian Political Leaders on anti-Muslim backlash' 19/9/2001 <http://www.muslimaffairs.com.au/News/PoliticalLeaders.htm> Download 18 October 2002

3. Statements of Federal politicians made on the opening of parliament (17/9/2001). Posted on the website of AMPAC 'News; Statements of Australian Political Leaders on anti-Muslim backlash' 19/9/2001 <http://www.muslimaffairs.com.au/News/PoliticalLeaders.htm> Download 18 October 2002

Chapter 14

1. Melanie Phillips, 'How the West was Lost', *Spectator*, May 11 2002. <http://pws.prserv.net/mpjr/mp/sp110502.htm> Downloaded 18 October 2002

INDEX